Permissible Advantage?

The Moral Consequences of Elite Schooling

Sociocultural, Political, and Historical Studies in Education
Joel Spring, Editor

Permissible Advantage?

The Moral Consequences of Elite Schooling

Alan Peshkin
Stanford University

LAWRENCE ERLBAUM ASSOCIATES, PUBLISHERS

2001   Mahwah, New Jersey   London

Lawrence Erlbaum Associates, Inc., Publishers
10 Industrial Avenue
Mahwah, NJ 07430

Cover art by Danny Silverman

Cover design by Kathryn Houghtaling Lacey

Library of Congress Cataloging-in-Publication Data

Peshkin, Alan.
Permissible advantage? : the moral consequences of elite
    schooling / Alan Peshkin.
        p.   cm.
Includes bibliographical references and index.
ISBN 0-8058-2466-9 (alk. paper) —
    ISBN 0-8058-2467-7 (pbk. : alk. paper)
1. Preparatory schools—Moral and ethical aspects—United
    States. 2. Preparatory schools—United States—Case
    studies. I. Title.
LC58.4 .P58 2000
373.2'22—dc21   00-037615
                                                          CIP

Printed in the United States of America
10 9 8 7 6 5 4 3 2 1

To my battalion

To say that the human condition is moral before it is or may be anything else means ... that whether we choose it or not, we confront our situation as a moral problem and our life choices as moral dilemmas. What follows is that we bear moral responsibilities ...

—Zygmunt Bauman (1995, p. 2)

Contents

Preface

This study of Edgewood Academy extends my ongoing exploration of American high schools. Each study has been centered in a different sociocultural setting. I began in rural, midwestern Mansfield and Mansfield High School (Peshkin, 1978/1994), where village life and agriculture were preeminent. I continued thereafter, first in fundamentalist Christian Bethany Baptist Academy (Peshkin, 1986), a school whose doctrinal orthodoxy shaped the education of true-believing students; next in blue-collar Riverview and Riverview High School (Peshkin, 1991), a multicultural community and school where the manifestation of ethnicity was central; and finally in Indian High School (Peshkin, 1997), a boarding school for Native American youth faced with the challenges of dual-world cultural commitment and competency.

Edgewood Academy, a nonpublic school, is a self-designated college preparatory institution. Its host community is not a village, town, church, or tribe, as in my previous studies. Its host is a community created by shared aspirations for high-level academic attainment and its associated benefits. In no previous study of mine were affluence and towering academic achievement relevant factors. I began this inquiry, as I did the others, with two questions that make sense in the context of these studies that I have been conducting since 1972. The questions were: First, what is a school like whose students enter with a determined disposition to attend college? To some degree, there are such students in all schools. At Edgewood Academy, all students fit this description. And, second, what can I learn from studying this school that transcends its particular circumstances? This question is in the spirit of Andrew Greeley's (1993) observation that "fiction and social research are both offsprings of the narrative impulse by which we humans strive to make sense of the world around us" (pp. 71–72). Making sense of the world does not readily transform into pedagogical difference in the near term. One hopes—an academic conceit?—that some good in some form may eventually occur, the possible result of a generative insight, perspective, or sensitivity. More certain, perhaps, is what a study of schools may reveal about the worlds that encompass them.

In this book, advantage occupies center stage, the star of my educational portrayal. Other stories can be told about Edgewood Academy; I don't tell them, at least not very thoroughly. I do not strive for a balanced account by which I would consider seriously the costs of advantage to those who participate in the Academy's venture, and to those who do not. Here and there I broaden the script, but my point always is what Edgewood Academy epitomizes to me. An Academy student, recounting a talk with his father, amply expresses my point:

> We are sending you to the Academy [his father told him] because it is a safe environment. We don't have to worry about gangs or shootings or any of what you consider harassment. I asked my dad, "Wasn't that kind of a little too sheltered, a little too separate from the outside world, kind of elite?" He said, "That is what we are paying for. We are paying for you to be around other smart kids, paying for the great futures."

What the Academy epitomizes is an array of moral choices that build on the enormous privilege of affluence. The implications of these choices extend internally to the school's promise of opportunity to its students and externally when these promises are viewed in the context of schooling for all American children.

Following a stage-setting first chapter, I describe (chaps. 2 through 5) what moral choices look like when they are made by the participants in an exceedingly wealthy school. Though I glance at the downside of things now and again, I often sound in these chapters as if I've been commissioned to write the school's publicity brochure. There is a general picture of Edgewood Academy (chap. 2); a discussion of the processes the school uses to ensure the quality of its students and educators (chap. 3); and an overview of teachers (chap. 4) and students (chap. 5) that reveals what is commendable about each group. These four chapters clarify what a school of ample financial means and wise leadership can do. In the second place, I pause briefly to reflect on privilege (chap. 6), before concluding in chapter 7 with a discussion of what the very existence of a privileged school indicates about American society. That schools are indicator institutions I suggest in the title of chapter 7—American Values. That is, schools are about more than just what goes on in them; they mirror what is and is not at stake for their particular constituents. They function similarly for the nation.

There is a book to write about Edgewood Academy as a school dedicated to the pursuit of excellence. In fact, most of this book describes the outcomes of this pursuit. However, I document the school's practices not to extol its success, but, rather, to use its success as the basis for calling attention to what is available for Academy youth that is not available for most American children. Thus, my focus is not on comprehensively documenting what goes on at Edgewood Academy, whether it should go on, and what changes have been made over the years in personnel, policy, and educational practice. Nor is it to contest the advantages that Edgewood Academy students acquire; I explore the permissibility of their advantages in the concluding chapter.

My focus, ultimately, is on educational justice as illuminated by the advantage of Academy students. If Jonathon Kozol (1991) in his *Savage Inequalities* depicts the particulars of educational justice denied, I depict a school where educational justice prevails. Like Kozol, my focus is on justice denied, though it is not because anyone or any group or agency consciously, planfully sets out to do injustice to other children. Rather, injustice happens as the artifact of imagined limitations of resources and means. As a nation, we more readily construe other priorities, problems, rationales, and justifications for sustaining educational injustice, than for overcoming it.

ACKNOWLEDGMENTS

As I prepare to identify those to whom I am indebted for being able to conduct this study and for better ways to say what I mean to say, as well as what I ought to say, I am reminded that each year, when I begin teaching, I remind students that the researcher's work is not done best as a solo performance. To say the least, this book is very far from such a performance.

I begin with my deepest and warmest expression of gratitude to Carol Kinney who provided me with a home away from home for all the years that I had contact with Edgewood Academy. Her hospitality and her company always reminded me that I had a life outside my work; I was pleased to be reminded. And I continue with equivalent gratitude to Shelley Roberts, who introduced me to her mother, Carol Kinney, facilitated my access to Edgewood Academy, and for years listened to my tales from the field of her New Mexican home.

Within Edgewood Academy, many educators, including one of its distinguished graduates, read all of my chapters and responded with marginal comments, general ideas, and good wishes. I needed all three. They reassured me that I had not done grave injustice to their school and, moreover, that I had said some things they thought needed saying. Moreover, I must add my appreciation for the wonderful cooperation I received during the academic year I spent at Edgewood Academy. I felt welcomed and always looked forward to my days spent in classrooms, at meetings and activities, and interviewing. Teachers, administrators, students, directors of admission, college counselors—all made possible the breadth and depth of what I learned. Thank you all.

Outside the Academy, I benefited, as I have for many years, from the comments of my wife, Maryann Peshkin, my long-time friend, Gordon Cohn, and my Illinois colleague of longest standing, Wally Feinberg. Ed Bridges and Mike Atkin from Stanford University also were generous with their time and observations devoted to my writing. I revised my manuscript on the basis of the suggestions and insights that all these fine readers provided me. And then I revised it again and again on the basis of exceptionally close, exceptionally useful readings by Art Powell, Denise Pope, and Sam Intrator.

I get by with a little help from my friends … and, most particularly, from the Spencer Foundation who generously funded my study. I am most grateful for their support.

—*Alan Peshkin*

1

A Moral Outlook

I

This is damn foolishness—it cannot be that the forty-ninth variety of bagel is more important than your schools ... and you ought to ask yourselves why you act as if it were ...

—*Robert Solow, Nobel Laureate*
(quoted in Cassidy, 1998), commenting on
Kenneth Galbraith's (1969) Affluent Society

Ⅰn America, it is illegal neither to create the forty-ninth variety of bagel nor to receive an education that is substandard compared to the best that others receive. But it is unfair, unjust, and unkind.

II

Advantage: "a factor or circumstance that gives superiority to its possessor or that puts him [her] ... in a favorable or improved position."

—*Webster's Third New International Dictionary (1966)*

Advantage surrounds me. I write from Stanford, California, a privileged "company" town that is redolent of physical, financial, and cultural well-being. I live down the street from Stanford University and Silicon Valley. The fabled Mediterranean climate brings year-round pleasure. The less advantaged live elsewhere.

By virtue of memory and contrast, my friend Cohn from Long Beach, California, often pulls me back to our ghetto on Chicago's West Side. It still is a ghetto today but for kids much less likely to eventually live favored lives elsewhere. The ghosts of my parents pull me back to Jane Addams' Hull House, which kept them off the street as children, and where I went for recreation each Saturday morning with my mother.

After seven, ten, maybe more false-start titles, I find *Permissible Advantage* to be the most fitting designation for this book about Edgewood Academy, an elite school, containing Grades 6 through 12, whose promise of outstanding educational opportunities and outstanding futures is eminently realizable. Edgewood Academy provides an educational experience and cachet that merits designation as *privileged*. The outcome of a privileged education is *advantage*, a relativistic term that indicates that Academy graduates have enhanced life opportunities compared to most students in the country.[1] Is it right that they do?

I find it interesting to think about advantage gained in biological terms, by which organisms seek advantage for their progeny in the selection of their mates. Similarly, Academy parents seek advantages for their children in their choice of schooling, which may represent a continuation of advantage seeking on the part of the parents and the initiation of advantage seeking on the part of their children. The lesson learned (or reinforced, as the case may be) is that choice of schooling is instrumental for keeping an already desirable status quo but also for changing an undesirable one.

I wanted to study a school where it was the norm that its students attended college, indeed, where it was a perverse act not to do so. Of necessity, this meant studying a school that served students with high educational and career aspirations. By good chance, I was introduced to and received permission to conduct research at Edgewood Academy,[2] a nonpublic school in New Mexico.

One does not drive by the school's otherwise residential neighborhood, located near the northeastern edge of the city, without taking note of the striking nonresidential structures that rise above their surroundings. The Academy could easily be mistaken for a small liberal arts college, with its spread of brick academic and administrative buildings, well-tended lawns and gardens,

---

[1] For the most part, the terms *privilege* and *advantage* can be used interchangeably, so that their usage comes down to points of personal preference and style.

[2] This is a pseudonym, as are the names of the students and educators I cite throughout the book.

array of playing fields, and imposing large library. The campus is bounded by a tall, black metal fence that encloses and separates the school from its surroundings. In this high desert region of New Mexico, a state known more for its beauty than its affluence, Edgewood Academy is both a physical and an educational oasis. It has its cultural origins in and connections to the opportunities and prospects of the larger world beyond its immediate location. A school is known by what it is designed to lead to, by what, in fact, it makes possible afterward for those whom it serves. A school is known by the nature and reach of advantage that its experience affords its students, and the Academy experience affords far-reaching advantages.

III

Over the years, professional and lay media have dealt with a variety of issues and forms of nonpublic schools. Twenty-five years ago, the proliferation of new Christian schools brought joy to many parents who saw the "humanist" public school as anathema to their doctrine, and despair to public school educators who saw a shrinking enrollment and corresponding decline in state revenues. On a smaller scale, African American and Hispanic Americans, also disappointed with public education, opened schools that would do educational justice to their cultural interests and needs. Further, interest in nonpublic (most often Catholic) schools arose—on grounds that were neither doctrinal nor cultural—from their possibly superior contribution to the academic achievement of urban students who otherwise did poorly in public schools.

This study of Edgewood Academy focuses on one type of nonpublic school—the elite school, known also by its primary function as a college preparatory school. My book differs from Arthur Powell's (1996) fine study that explores "the education that privileged schools provide and not privilege itself" (p. 6). The latter is more my focus. It also differs from Peter Cookson and Caroline Persell's (1985) work that concludes by wondering if the "prep experience" has become so outmoded that we should look, rather, "to those who are less shackled by conventional ways of doing things," to those who are less "prisoners of their class" (p. 207). Perhaps because it is not a boarding school, and because it is a relatively new school located in the more egalitarian southwest, Edgewood Academy's students show no sign of shackling or being class prisoners.

Clearly, there is a host of conceivable focal points in the study of elite schools. Many of them already have been incorporated in existing literature:

• Legal issues (Devins, 1989)

- a rationale for their existence (Heely, 1951)
- pedagogical lessons (Powell, 1996)
- the economic advantages of their students (Bills, 1988; Collins, 1979; and Kingston, 1981)
- reproduction of elites (Cookson & Persell, 1985; Maxwell & Maxwell, 1995)
- enhanced access to elite higher education (Cookson & Persell, 1985)
- identity formation (Proweller, 1998)
- historical analysis (McLachlan, 1970)
- comparative academic achievement (Haertel, James, & Levin, 1987)
- tuition tax credits and governance structures (James & Levin, 1988)
- minority student attendance (Doyle, 1981)
- moral traditions (Hays, 1994).

There is more; this list is suggestive of the topics and literature available to illuminate the working of elite nonpublic schools.

IV

Morris Dickstein (1996) wrote that Congress's "diminished sympathy for society's losers" can be traced to several factors, "but some of it arises from a willed ignorance of how the other half lives. Because we all lead insular lives ... the poor remain part of a distant underclass and take on no individual reality" (p. 19). Dickstein is right about our so-called losers, but his point extends equally to our so-called winners, who enjoy a corresponding oversight. Anthropologist Laura Nader (1969) reminded us of the disproportionate focus of researchers on the poor and the powerless, as did Lois Weis and Michele Fine (1991), who stress that we should not forget those institutions embodying historical power—the private secondary school. This oversight tends to preclude us from asking who the winners are and what they are walking away with.

Privilege and *advantage* operate as my controlling concepts, the filtering terms that shaped what I saw and what I care to write about. Zygmunt Bauman's (1995) point about our moral responsibilities leads to an admonition that only the most depraved would deny. Of course, we have moral responsibilities, a cost-free concession. Moving beyond this concession is where everything becomes moot and where our accord gets lost, then abandoned, in the deep morass of Who gets how much? Who decides? and What next?

All school decisions are moral in nature because in one way or another, sooner or later, they relate to the well-being (e.g., political, economic, cognitive, emotional, social) of students, parents, community, and society. Of procedural importance are questions such as: Who, in fact, makes the judgments—

pedagogical, curricular, organizational, and interpersonal—that determine what the nature of the school will be, and who does not? Who are the beneficiaries of these decisions? Whose good do they ignore or slight or undermine? And do they take account of the short-, middle-, and long-term needs and aspirations of students?

Of substantive importance is the outcome of decisions made about what schools elect to teach; what form teaching takes; what ideological orientation is given to what is taught; and what resources are provided for the efficacy of what is taught. "Education," as Chris Clark (1991) observed, "is a profoundly moral business" (p. 431; see also Dewey, 1909; Jackson, Boostrom, & Hansen, 1993; Tom, 1984).

I am attracted to the perspective provided by moral choice because of our conventional concern as a society for what is moral, albeit a concern that is much more often associated with religion than with education, more often with the Girl Scouts than with the glee club. Behavior considered moral, outcomes considered moral—as a people, we take these matters to be salient and essential, perhaps inevitably so (Kagan, 1998). If only for the sake of appearances, we learn that we should not demean what others take to be moral. By focusing on moral choices, I underscore that while on the face of it, schools are about algebra and accounting, basketball and drama, field trips and competitions, they are, as well, most fully, inevitably, and irrevocably about what is moral. As such, what schools do and what happens in school must never be taken lightly, for all this goes to the heart of our lives.

Furthermore, the mere existence of particular types of schools—doctrinally suffused Christian schools, ethnically centered schools, or academically oriented, elite prep schools—indicate moral choices that some American subgroup has made and, moreover, that American society has made about legally acceptable ways to educate American children.

Some moral choices that affect schools originate in the action of state legislatures and state departments of education, some in the financial and regulatory stipulations that emerge from federal government action. Day-to-day, however, a school's moral choices originate in and are enacted by the ongoing action of its local clientele and community. In fact, as an embedded institution (Peshkin, 1995), schools are subject to an enormous number and type of agencies—e.g., interest groups, think tanks, professional organizations—desirous of having their particular moral choices imposed on the schools, choices that embody their version of appropriate values. Because schools are assumed to be important for individual and collective well-being, they always will be subject to the wishes and wishful thinking of internal and external agencies. Such agencies see their success, comfort, prosperity, *ad infinitum*, at stake if something in our schools is not removed, added, or modified in a specified way.

As less embedded institutions, nonpublic schools enjoy the relative ease of fewer constituent groups that assume prerogatives to shape the moral choices these schools must make. Ostensibly, the most immediate agents with a stake in the Academy's moral choices and their outcomes are its clients, the parents and their children; its educators; and its board of trustees. This said, I will not explicate the positions and preferences of these agents, noting where they overlap and where they contend.

V

In his journey to "London slum life" at the end of the 19th century, George Sims wrote: "I commence with the first of these chapters, a book of travel … I propose to record the result of a journey into a region which lies at our own doors—into a dark continent that is within easy walking distance of the General Post Office" (quoted in Parssinen, 1982, p. 205).

I felt I had undertaken a distant journey when I set out to learn about Edgewood Academy, not to a dark but surely, for me, to an unknown "continent." Indeed, I often felt like a voyeur when I strolled the tree-shaded walks from one part of the campus to the other, ate lunch family-style with teachers and students at round tables for ten, and saw the impact of the school's affluence reflected in its provisions for every part of its academic life. It was as if I had been transported by television to the school life of the rich and famous. And I stayed behind when the show was over to peek into the daily affairs of the less than 1% of American children who manage to attend such schools.

(I must digress for a moment to note that as I write these words I continually am struck by the singularity of what I have learned about Edgewood Academy; it inspires superlatives that once acquired do not fade with the acquisition of further information. Accordingly, I keep feeling tempted to append to a statement I have made, or that I have quoted someone else as saying, such comments as, "This can be said about few schools anywhere" or "The Academy is virtually alone in this or that regard." I add this digression to clarify my state of mind—both as I collected information and as I write this book. Succinctly stated, in many important regards, the Academy has few peers.)

My research journey to Edgewood Academy contrasts strikingly with my journeys to other schools of choice. At Bethany Baptist Academy, I resided with a family of local church members and lived as if I was a Christian in regard to the fullest possible participation in all ongoing church activities. At Indian High School, I lived at a distance from the reservation homes of most of the students, a necessity mandated by the determined intent of Pueblo Indians to keep their theocratic communities apart from the gaze of outsiders. At

Edgewood Academy, I felt at home in the way I do in university settings, where I have lived almost all of my life. Although I felt at home, I never lost the dual sense the school evoked in me, that of the admiring "look what these students are getting," and that of the despairing "look what other students are not." This duality provides the primary impetus for writing this book.

Yet, my wish that all children could attend schools like the Academy falters before the recollection of a rural school district I studied some years ago (Peshkin, 1982). The citizens of "Killmer," Illinois, rallied to oppose the school board's closing of their beloved village school. They rejected the nearby school to which their children would have been bused, a school that they, and everyone else involved, acknowledged as educationally superior. To Killmer parents one might say, "You don't know what's good." To which they might reply, "But we know what we like." There is an important issue here: whose perspective should prevail—that of educational professionals, politicians, local tax payers, or parents? The issue is unsettled.

The ostensible fact of educational inequality does not predictably motivate for redress. For inequality becomes familiar and normalized. It is palpably present on every surface and within every interstice of American society. It is manifest in the distribution of space, time, material, food, air, service, health, opportunity, comfort, knowledge, cleanliness, money, and hope. Evidence of inequalities is graphically apparent by what people wear, drive, eat, and breathe; by where they live, play, earn a living; and, my case in point, by how they are educated.

Academy parents would scoff at the preferences of Killmer parents; indeed, they might question their sanity. For they have chosen an academic epitome for their children, and nothing less will suffice. It is the school's and their own personal fortunes, not tax dollars, that enable this school's existence. They are pleased with a prep-American curriculum that exalts hard work, striving, competition, achievement, and success; along the way, there is poetry, the arts, higher order thinking skills, verbal accomplishment, and high test scores. All of this is congruent with the home culture of most Academy students. It is congruent, as well, as the means to the end of acquiring compelling advantage for life beyond the Academy. Parents celebrate the fit between their dreams for their children (and themselves), and what their chosen school can deliver. To provide the means for all parents everywhere to have a dream and to celebrate such a fit strikes me as the proper starting point for all educational policy.

2

Circumstances of Education

Were Samuel Pepys a member of the Visiting Committee, most certainly he would exclaim, "It is pretty to see what money can do."

—*External Evaluation Committee*

WELCOME TO EDGEWOOD ACADEMY

In 1988, a team of external examiners visited Edgewood Academy, a private high school in the independent tradition,[1] for the purpose of assessment as required by the National Association of Independent Schools (NAIS). Clearly, this team, bent on ascertaining the merit of Edgewood Academy, admired what it had observed and studied over the course of several days. They were not being sardonic. Their point was not the school's enormous affluence but how well they thought it was being put to use. At Edgewood Academy, it *is* "pretty to see what money can do."

---

[1]For a useful general picture of independent schools see Pearl Rock Kane's (1991) article, "Independent Schools in American Education." She informs us that there are 1,500 such schools in the United States and that they are distinguished by six attributes that she elaborates: "self-governance, self-support, self-defined curriculum, self-selected students, self-selected faculty, and small size" (p. 397).

—

In 1925, the U.S. Supreme Court ruled in *Pierce v. Society of Sisters* that private schools have a right to exist and parents have a right to choose them as alternatives to public school ...

—*Kemerer* (1992, p. 56)

The Supreme Court's 1925 ruling grew out of a case involving a Catholic school. At the time, the country was unfriendly both to Catholics and their desire to avoid having their children educated in public schools that struck Catholics as overly Protestant in character. The country, then as now, however, was not unfriendly to the elite private school, denominational or not, boarding or not. These well-established, well-protected institutions—the Andovers and the Choates—were historically associated with the nation's wealthy, who saw little promise in public education and considerable opportunity in schools that only they could afford. Edgewood Academy is a contemporary version of such a school, of the nondenominational, nonboarding variety. It enjoys the fruits of educational precedent. Secured by legal decision, it serves one group that never even considers the public school as a possible alternative, and another that is escaping the limits it sees in the public school.

Alan Peshkin   Do your parents believe that you get something here that you
(AP):   can't get at the public schools?

Student: Yes. They want you to be on the top of the food chain. They want us to be the bosses, not the employees. They want us to be the people who get the high wages. They want us to be in charge. We are going to be the leaders.

This voice of personal advantage, drawn from the student's assessment of his parent's values, is unadorned by mitigating reference to outcomes of higher order thinking skills, intellectual independence, or equal opportunity. It is bare-bones cynicism, the observations of a junior boy who enjoys academic, athletic, and social success.

INDEPENDENT SCHOOLS

Schools like Edgewood Academy have designations derived from what they are and from what they are not. From the latter category, Edgewood Academy is a *nondenominational, nonpublic* school. Given that most nonpublic schools are denominational (overwhelmingly Catholic, followed by fundamentalist Christian, and a relative smattering of other Christian, Jewish, and Muslim schools), the designation as nondenominational has meaning. *Nonpublic* departs from the majority school category of public, and simply lumps the Academy with every other type of nonpublic school. *Public*, the key word, refers to a school's primary source of funding,[2] to its mythic mission as the school for all the children of all the people, and to its governance. Public speaks to the putative obligation of schools to the public good.

The label *private* includes every type of school whose founders seek the prerogative to determine whom to admit, whom to hire, what to teach, how to teach, and what to emphasize. Private designates institutions whose founders believe their mission cannot be served by a public institution. Their primary goals may be incongruent with those of all public schools (as in religious schools), or, possibly, with particular public schools (as in the racist, segregationist academies of the South).

From this same category comes the designation *independent*. This is Edgewood Academy's preferred identity, a designation incorporated in its professional association (National Association of Independent Schools), and a reference to its hoped-for distance from the sources of political, educational, and financial control that apply to public schools.

Finally, Edgewood Academy is a college preparatory or *prep* school, the label most meaningful to parents and children who above all seek preparedness for successful competition in the elite worlds of further schooling and work.

Each of the aforementioned five ways of categorizing the Academy raises a certain question: As a nondenominational school, we can ask what, then, are its underlying beliefs; as a nonpublic school, we can ask what its commitment is to the public good; as a private school, we can ask about the forms of its exclusivity; as an independent school, we can ask what it has done with its freedom; and as a prep school, we can ask about the academic and other costs of a school whose existence is so immediately tied to getting and staying ahead. These questions are the context for coming to grips with the Academy's most salient attribute as an elite school that embodies and fosters educational privilege, an outcome enhanced by, but not dependent on, its status as an independent school.

Elaborating on what being an independent school entails will clarify several of the defining features of these schools. The independent school stands apart from community and state control, as far apart as it can, in order to be free to shape a school in the interests of a particular constituency, unfettered by the curricular constraints that operate for public schools. So, what is independent about an independent school? "We are not dictated by a governmental or state agency, or even a local agency, for curriculum," answers an Academy teacher. "We have the opportunity to try different things." Although unavoidably subject to state health and safety requirements, independent schools strive to re-

---

[2]It no longer is true that nonpublic schools are funded only by nonpublic sources. Several types of nonpublic schools eagerly seek and accept public money.

main free of state requirements for teacher certification, maintaining, often vociferously, that a null relationship exists between teacher certification and teacher effectiveness:

> I don't know if you've ever taken educational courses, Alan, but they're just so cut and dried. You have to jump through hoops, and there's no psychology in them. It's all purely methods and organization. The way to learn how to teach is to just do it. Everyone's first year is just hell because of that.

This view is widespread at Edgewood Academy.

Independent schools are also independent of the necessity of retaining either the students they have admitted or the teachers they have hired.

> I remember a parent conference I had. Oh God, this guy starts pounding on the table, yelling, "Why aren't you giving my son better grades?" The headmaster was in the meeting. He finally said, "You know, if we are making you so unhappy, why don't you just withdraw your child." That guy changed his tune real quickly. That's our ultimate threat.

In the usual absence of tenure and of teachers' unions to defend teacher rights, independent school teachers can be dismissed more readily than public school teachers.

> I know I'm very fortunate to teach here because I know that I can do what I want to do. I have the means to use my creativity and my teaching ability. There is pressure that comes with it. I have a one-year contract renewed every year. I've had fifteen one-year contracts.

Independent schools are independent of regulations that require them to accept any students other than those they declare have satisfied their own standards, or to confine hiring teachers to the pool of those legitimated by state certification. These options, together with the following facts, give these schools their particular form (see also Conway, 1992): The independent school is likely, overall, to be small, have low student–teacher ratios, and draw students from wealthier families (in 1993, 58 percent of families in nonsectarian schools had incomes over $35,000 compared to 41% in church-related schools and 27% in public schools (*Myths and Facts about Private School Choice*, 1993, n. p.).

The median tuition for NAIS member day schools in the 1991–1992 school year was $6,928; for NAIS member boarding schools, it was $15,867. Academy students in 1991–1992, the school year for which my data apply, unless otherwise specified, paid a tuition of $5,950, an additional $575 for lunch, and approximately $150 to $250 more for books. The Academy subsidized each student's education by an amount equal approximately to the tuition; annual per pupil costs were about $13,000. By 1994–1995, the annual tuition was $6,950 and annual per pupil costs were $15,000. Some perspective on the magnitude of this latter figure derives from information on one of the most academically sound and wealthy public schools in the nation—Winnetka, Illinois' New Trier High School, whose per pupil expenditures were $9,011.

Independent schools have acquired an ideal-type stature of strong, wise leadership from headmasters of storied fame; a pervasive sense of community among students and educators based on shared mission and deserved pride in academic and other achievements (see Deal, 1992); classrooms of rich intellectual exchange that more resemble the engaging activity of the small liberal arts college than of the American high school; and polymath teachers who can move from sterling accomplishment as pedagogues to inspired guidance as soccer coaches. That this ideal type has few full-fledged embodiments in the flesh does not preclude Academy teachers from marveling over the wonders of independent schools, including, at its best, their own:

> There are schools all over the country that are getting things done because there is a principal in charge who simply accepts that his or her responsibility is that something happens in that damn place every day. Everybody contributes to it. And the people who don't contribute, she finds out why and she serves notice: You either put up or you move out. She creates a climate where things are happening and the ne'er-do-wells will leave. They don't have to be pushed out.

The independent school also can be seen in several lights, each underscoring a different dimension of the same school, and each dimension attached to a different notion of what basically the school entails. Observes psychiatrist Robert Coles, whose own children have attended independent schools:

> [W]hat is the independent school but a social version of privilege? It's a school devoted to those who have the means and the wish to separate themselves from others and get a kind of education that presumably is distinctive and better ... Most of us think of independent schools as centers of privilege. (Coles, 1992, p. 276)

Observes an Academy teacher:

> There's an incredible stigma attached to independent schools being a place for rich kids. [But] I think today, more so than ever before, we're not a place for rich kids. We're a place for kids who want to excel academically and to feel comfortable, who won't have other obstacles with respect to classroom management and social climate of the school that will prevent them from doing that.

Center of privilege, center for academic excellence: Is each view true? Yes. One truer than the other? This is a matter of perspective. One of more moment than the other for uncovering what the Academy reveals about American society? Yes, as Coles would see it.

BASIC FACTS

Edgewood Academy and its brethren address the world of potential new student recruits with documents designed to put a true best foot forward. I will selectively cite from the school's brochure. In the 1990s, Edgewood Academy's enrollment of about 900 students is many more than the handful who came to the new, untested school at its opening in 1955 as a school for boys in blue blazers. (The school is now coeducational and the students do not wear uniforms.) Ten years later, the first of many new buildings would be built on its current 312 acre main campus. Another 270 nearby mountain acres are available for an array of school-linked activities organized within a program called "experiential education." I had an office in the science building for the year I was there, testimony to the amplitude of office space in a school where each teacher has a private office, complete with personal computer and comfortable office trappings, and testimony to the thoughtfulness of the school's headmaster, Ed Compton.

The school took particular pride in the accomplishments spelled out in one succinct paragraph in the brochure:

> The Academy seeks a highly talented, motivated and diverse student body ... 48% of our students are female, 25% are students of color, and 30% are receiving more than $1,200,000 in financial aid. Financial aid is based entirely on demonstrated financial need.

The brochure ends with a profile of the graduating class: 27% received National Merit recognition, 12% were semifinalists, 15% received letters of commendation, and 6% were Hispanic scholar semifinalists. Mean SAT scores were verbal 539, math 613 (compared to 500 and 501, respectively, in the nation overall); the mean composite ACT score was 27. Of 415 advanced placement examinations taken by 198 students, 38% received scores of 4 or 5; the top score is 5. The brochure's concluding celebration was that "Approximately 99% of Academy graduates enroll in 4-year colleges immediately after graduation, and follow-up studies indicate that, on average, Academy graduates earn higher academic averages as college freshmen than they did as Academy students."

Prospective students and their families are thereby reassured, if any reassurance at this time in the school's history is needed, that Edgewood Academy delivers on its promise as a prep school. Its graduates gain honors and are admitted to worthy colleges and universities where, on average, they do very well.

ADMINISTERING EDGEWOOD ACADEMY

Appropriate committees of the board continue to monitor carefully all invested assets ranging from highly marketable securities ... to the less liquid but diversified investments in the real estate and private placement markets.

—*Board of Trustees, Annual Report*

In keeping with the independent school tradition, the Academy's top administrator is a "headmaster" who is responsible to a Board of Trustees. The headmaster–board relationship and division of labor vary from school to school. Headmaster Compton, by his design, is unusually autonomous. He is the school's executive officer, answerable to the Board that meets at least five times per year. In their private capacities, the men and women of the Board are in medicine, the law, and business; typically, they have or had children who attend the Academy. Several were former Academy students.

The Board of Trustees rests atop a sizable administrative structure that demonstrates the complexity of Edgewood Academy: by its range of commitments (Director of Summer School, Director of Summer Camps); by its sensitivity to financial matters (Chief Business and Financial Officer); and by the specialized leadership services (Director of Computer Services, Director of Day Camp, Director of Software Instruction). What no administrative table can show is how leadership actually works, particularly that part of it encompassing the school's curricular aspect. While Headmaster Compton is in charge of day-to-day operations, he delegates considerable responsibility to his deans and department chairs so that he can be relatively free to attend to what he sees as the larger, less immediate issues of school direction, planning, and finance, except as more immediate issues become problematic and command his attention. Listen to the words of one department chair commenting on his sense of Compton's position:

> The Head has done an astonishing thing here. He has created departments that are preposterously potent in their roles. The head has steadfastly eschewed micromanagement. He has tacitly said, "Here, have all the rope in the world to build the most magnificent single-span suspension bridge, or to construct a perfect noose for yourself."

Headmaster Compton is an honest, forthright man. He knows and declares what he values, and is not inclined to shape his preferences to suit the particular audience before him. On a bright Saturday morning in early September, senior students meet with Compton for a weekend retreat. Dressed in shorts as befits the informality of the setting, students are sprawled around a large room. The questions students raise challenge not so much what decisions the school has made but how they were made, notably that their voices were not heard.

Compton remains calm and undefensive; he does not placate. Students cannot mistake his meaning.

> Some of what you see now comes from plans made with student input when you were in the middle school. More emphasis obviously has been given to faculty input. For certain decisions, it would be cosmetic to ask your opinion. You don't have the background. I don't believe in charades. When you can be appropriate, ok; when not, not. True, everything affects you, but take the decision about having an orchard. That does not affect you on a day-to-day basis. We need the nursery to raise our own plants. Some decisions are beyond you. I know that does not sound good, but do you have the time to participate? I think not. [A student comments, "With all the change going on, where is the school going? It feels like a carnival ride."] We have been free to act on our dreams. Our long-range plan of 1987 has been largely implemented. It mostly related to physical plant. This is a year of planning for the next 4 to 5 years. We won't know what it'll bring. I hope it will include an openness to new ideas, to admitting we've done wrong. Part of the future will include hearing from you. We will continue to be dynamic and vital.

Compton's words about a "year of planning" and the student's about a "carnival ride" will be borne out by committees put in place and by faculty reactions to what feels like a whirlwind of change. For among the facts that distinguish Edgewood Academy and Headmaster Compton is that the school has the means to implement the plans it makes, and the headmaster has the will and the leadership to see that plans are implemented. At schools everywhere, a certain cynicism is born on the heels of repeated plans from internal and external sources that fail to advance beyond the status of words. Not so at Edgewood Academy, where words become deeds. When its teachers say, "Here we go again," it is not a reaction to things once more undone, but once more to too much being done, as they see it.[3]

I did not hear Compton speaking with a comparable group of parents, but in the course of my interviews with him, I asked him about parents. To be sure, it is easier to put matters straight while speaking with me in the privacy of his paneled office than with parents in a publicly assembled group. I am convinced, however, that what he tells me, he would tell anyone. He is not a man of hidden agendas or obfuscation. Headmaster Compton has nothing to hide. Given the courage of his convictions, he clearly expresses his intentions and expectations:

---

[3]Teachers found the dizzying pace of change to be unsettling. A combination of physical (new buildings),administrative (new persons appointed to new positions), structural (a complicated timetable), and curricular (new courses) changes undercut the teachers' need for order, predictability, and community. Widespread, successful change, paradoxically, proved to be too much of a good thing.

Those parents largely from the public sector are used to—unhealthy in my view—involvement in determining what books kids will read, what plays they are going to see or produce, and so on. I try very carefully to tell parents there is a fine line: "Look, here is what we are doing. If you have any concerns, call us and let us know. Clearly, we don't pretend to have a patent on all the good ideas, but what you have to know is that in the final analysis, it is in fact the faculty's responsibility to make educational decisions, not the parents'." I think part of what makes us strong is in fact that we have only ourselves as a faculty to convince what is worth asking our students to do. And if we are able to convince ourselves, we jolly well should be able to convince the students and the parents.

Our parents are successful. They are where they are by winning most of the time, not by losing. So, there is a kind of competitive side to them, a very hardnosed side with some that can make it hard to deal with them. They are there, they are always there, and you kind of feel it. I don't find it overwhelming.

No school is independent in the sense of being unanswerable to any authority other than itself. As noted, Headmaster Compton reports to the Trustees, but in no formal sense do they represent parents or a community of taxpayers in the way that an elected public school board does. Without tenure, Compton governs, as his teachers teach, at the pleasure of the Trustees; ultimately, he answers to them and the teachers to him, but with an understanding that pedagogical matters rest "in the final analysis" within his and his educators' purview. Parents, being tuition payers and who they are, comment, complain, and argue. They are not, however, a public to which the school must be responsive in the usual way. They choose the Academy, and the Academy chooses their child. In the event that these choices prove to be the wrong ones, the child leaves, either by parental or school decision. The Academy offers the fruits of its pedagogical decisions and expertise to its clients. What exactly these offerings should embrace is a matter of ongoing discussion among Academy educators, whose work is framed by a mission statement included in several documents disseminated to Academy students, parents, and educators.

GOOD WORDS: MISSION POSSIBLE?

While we understandably remain a community of competitive individuals, I [the Board president] believe the goal of high achievement is pursued these days much less at the expense of others.

—Board of Trustees, Annual Report

I think the mission of the school—I mean, you can read the mission statement—but I think our real mission is to be on the cutting edge of education ...

—Academy teacher

The good words of a school, grandly termed its "mission statement," should inspire and direct the thought and energy of all those associated with the school. If accepted, these words can mobilize educators so that their otherwise disparate efforts can be focused to achieve desired outcomes. Although educators may adopt variant classroom strategies, their contributions ought to converge upon guiding ideas that will unite them in a shared enterprise. Under the best of circumstances, all members of a school community pull together, the school's mission a beacon that clarifies its direction and the point of departure to which all return.

Of course, Edgewood Academy has a mission statement. Indeed, all schools have the equivalent of one under the headings of school aims, purposes, goals, or objectives. I don't recall ever reading any such statement that did not specify sterling qualities for its students to acquire. Most often, the statements are the products of occasion—external visitors of some sort are coming in an evaluative capacity and they must be shown a statement of school purpose. Less often, they are products of moment—shared words and meanings that have grown out of the actual desires and abilities of a school's educators.

Academy documents prepared for students, parents, and faculty contain the three headings Mission Statement, Our Mission, and A Statement of Philosophy. Underneath the different headings are these identical words:

> Edgewood Academy's principal objective is the academic, creative, moral and physical development of each student. ... Emphasis is placed upon students developing sound scholarship, mastering the fundamentals on which higher learning is based, and developing independence of thought, cooperative self-reliance and discriminating judgment. ... In sum, the Academy seeks to prepare its graduates to serve their country and communities with wisdom and conviction, and their fellow beings with compassion.

Although other schools might reorder the textual location and thereby the suggested priority of these many outcomes, they could not easily object to them. Good words may never go out-of-date, but over time their meanings can erode so that new language must be created that recaptures their sense. As school leadership changes, teachers change, and society changes, mission statements can become mere linguistic shells, their good sound misleading the unwary who have not realized that a preponderance of change has eviscerated their meaning. In any event, the prevailing practices of a school are the operating reality that frame a school's mission. At Edgewood Academy, there is no better starting point for grasping its prevailing dynamic than Headmaster Compton.

A few weeks after the school year begins, Compton meets with all new teachers. Teachers are arrayed at two sets of long tables. They listen intently. Compton is their boss; moreover, he is an engaging speaker. His intent, I infer, is to give these newcomers an overview of the school, its students, and its commitments, which are his commitments, to be sure, but not only his. That for which Compton is the architect both reflects and builds on the commitments of his faculty. His talk touches a number of points. *Students*—he characterizes them as "high energy, aggressive, and curious, all qualities that we cultivate." *Quality*—"We have the potential to do great things in education. We are imperfect, but we admit it and settle for nothing less than perfection." *Faculty development*—"Few institutions devote more resources to faculty development. You are committed to growth by the terms of your contract. One of my perversities is you should not be thinking of summer as summer vacation. This is a time to do serious professional work—travel, reading, study. You can't accept employment elsewhere without my approval. No one will become rich working here, but you make fifty percent more than elsewhere." *Diversity*—"We are committed to diversity in teaching and learning styles, gender, ethnicity, socioeconomic status. No other objective carries with it more risk of failure. Diversity makes it hard to reach consensus." Later in the school year, when Compton speaks to the parents of new, incoming students, he reiterates what he said to the new teachers, commenting that values need to be lived, not just preached, and that the Academy "daily needs to model empathy, trust, altruism, cooperation, fairness, justice, and compassion."

Compton depicts a school characterized by energy, striving, and high expectations directed toward perfection. "Settling for nothing less than perfection" could be construed as Napoleonic bombast, the inflated rhetoric of headmaster-as-big-time-coach, hyperbole to inspire but not to be taken literally. A year of listening to his faculty and administrators—often one and the same person at independent schools where the tradition is that everyone teaches—persuades me that Compton's words are to be taken seriously. It is perhaps a mark of fine administrators to say only what they mean should be taken seriously.

It is the mark of a school whose personnel are in touch with each other when what the head of the school means seriously, the faculty takes seriously. Academy educators seem more comfortable with a term other than "perfection" to describe the school's quality of striving. For example, they speak of the Academy's "obligation" to serve as a model of what can "happen in education," not only for the state but also for the nation. All teachers do not adopt this degree of identification with Headmaster Compton's perception of the grand place of the Academy in American education. However, few fail to accept that the "pursuit of excellence," broadly stated, is a fair and realistic appraisal of the school's intent, some being specific about it as a "Compton thing" and, thus, "that there is something behind it that is pretty real" because it comes from him. What elsewhere might be uttered with disdain or cynicism, is not at the Academy. "There is like a mania to do the best we can."

While no one can or does protest the worthiness of "academic, creative, moral and physical development," Academy educators, unsurprisingly, perform a multitude of acts in the name of these educational objectives. Could it be otherwise, not least with teachers as carefully selected as the Academy's? And not least when there is an Academy standard, advocated by some teachers, that views the school's mission not in terms of student outcomes but in terms of a type of teacher: "find really extraordinary, gifted people who will excite children's minds and hearts and souls." Another teacher says in this regard, "What is the [school's] mission? Find exciting teachers to teach these kids, who will churn them up, get them excited about something during the course of their education."

Other teachers locate the school's mission in particular subject matter accomplishments:

> When students graduate from here they're going to be versed in a foreign language, able to speak and write English well, relatively knowledgeable in science, have enough mathematics to survive in the world, and know enough history to be able to place themselves.

Teacher emphasis on accomplishment in academic subject matter is congruent with emphasis on the employment of superlative teachers, as it is with their seeing the school's mission in terms of student conduct. For example, that students should become "engaged learners and questioners"; be "comfortable with complexity, intellectually and socially and emotionally and every other way"; learn "not to be the prisoners of unexamined axioms"; and be "able to see things from more viewpoints." Such a list is easily extended. Academy teachers are accustomed to articulating what they and their school should try to attain. When they step away from the school's formal mission statement, about whose vague generality they may be somewhat reserved, they attest to concerns that represent some fusion of personal values, a sense of what behaviors it takes to master their subject, and necessary behavior for conduct in the world beyond school.

Students anywhere could be forgiven for drawing a blank if asked about their school's mission, or, less technically, about what their school is trying to achieve. Like most everyone else at Edgewood Academy, however, students are verbally adept. I ask in so many words, what is your school up to? "I think to be just a thinking person. Being able to have some confidence in yourself. You're not just taking what's spoonfed to you. You want to question what's going into your head." And, "I don't think they want you to memorize facts. They want you to learn how to learn." And in language that seems to leaps straight from a Headmaster Compton script:

> *AP:* In an overall sense, is the Academy trying to develop you to be some particular kind of person?

Student: Yeah. They try to make you perfect.

AP: Perfect! Are you kidding?

Student: I don't know. I mean, if you like did everything they told you, you would be like the perfect person. I guess they want you to be the well-rounded, Renaissance-type person.

AP: Does anyone use that language?

Student: No, but I just thought of that from history class. You are always trying different things and picking different ways. Besides that, they put a lot of emphasis on college, making you the perfect college student.

A PLACE OF QUALITY

People talk about changing jobs and moving and things, but I would put off anything I want to do so my kids can go to this school because I think it's so good.

—Academy parent

I see these kids who come out of the Academy get scholarships, get financial aid, and are well qualified to get into very good colleges. That is why I started grooming my daughter at the pre-school level, to give her the best possible education I could to get her in here ... How much pressure do I put on her in the next 3 years to create this super child?

—Aspiring Academy parent

The world at Edgewood Academy that I try to make sense of inspires many parents to eulogize, if not to glorify. Behind the laudatory language is what is normal at this school, that is, what students and teachers and staff have come to expect as the ordinary fare of an ordinary day, what they wake up daily to find when they drive through the open gates of the fence that surrounds the school, walk down the campus paths and building corridors, and arrive in their classrooms and wherever else the normal activity of the school occurs. What is normal at the Academy merits laurels aplenty. Since the arrival of Headmaster Compton, the laurels may be evoked as points of pride, announced in its documents of public display, but not rested on. The Academy's normal is vibrant, a dynamic mingling of plans and energy, resolve and aspiration. In every school's composite of normal activities are the possibilities and opportunities that students and educators may experience. In this section I address some of the elements and attributes of this composite.

Facilities

To accommodate its approximately 900 students, Edgewood Academy has six classroom buildings, two libraries, a fine arts center (containing a theater, auditorium, and art gallery), and a sports complex of three gymnasiums, two football fields, four soccer fields, three baseball diamonds, sixteen tennis courts, and a nine-lane, all-weather track.

To illustrate Academy facilities at their most impressive, I will present the library, newly opened in 1991.

> The amazing thing about this place was that they [the administration] said, "We want the best," and that includes the best architects, whoever and wherever they are. So we interviewed many architects. We got proposals from twenty that we had preselected. Then we narrowed from there and visited them in their home offices. We split it up. I took the east coast, somebody else took the west coast, somebody took Florida.

This is the head librarian speaking of the library's origin in a search that took her and others around the country. Rich schools are not restricted to local resources. She saw it designed and built, and now enjoys and operates a service that employs 9 persons, including herself; 4 of the nine work half-time and 5 work full-time; 35 parent volunteers each contribute 3 hours per week to the work of the salaried staff.

The library is open to Academy students and their families, to former students, and to current faculty and staff, including their families. Here are the details of the library's availability to its patrons, which details I have never before thought worthy of inclusion in anything I have written about any other school. During the school year, the library of this day school is open 7:30 a.m.–9:00 p.m., Monday through Thursday, and 7:30 a.m.–4:00 p.m. on Friday; it is closed on Saturday, but open again on Sunday, 1:00 p.m.–9:00 p.m. During the summer, it is open Monday to Friday, 8:00 a.m.–3:00 p.m. Edgewood Academy raises to new heights the meaning of an open school library.

Within this expansive time frame of availability librarians see their dreams fulfilled: an on-line catalog of the material in its own library and the material in the nearby major state university; access to thousands of libraries throughout the country; and an annual budget of $150,000, which includes periodicals, books, audiovisual materials, microfiche machines, etc.[4] Another $7,000 per year comes from contributions parents make on the occasion of their child's birthday.

Curriculum

One week before Christmas, the faculty and students who comprise the school's Educational Policy Committee received a packet containing descrip-

---

[4]The librarian estimates that the annual library budget of public schools ranges from $6,000 to $8,000.

tions of 28 new courses for introduction in the next academic year. They join the large list of courses already available. Unsurprisingly, Academy students can choose from a wide array of elective courses, so that they can take what amounts to a major, for example, in science, history, or the visual arts. The 28 new courses replace some old courses, but mostly they add to the already rich curricular choice.

From these 28 proposals, we learn that *English* will be joined by the newly approved Advanced Grammar and Vocabulary: "After a solid review, the class will go beyond regular English studies into intriguing grammatical forms. Root forms (Greek, Latin, etc.) will provide the foundation for vocabulary growth"; *history* by Who's Talking: Media, Propaganda and Knowledge in Today's Society: "Students will ... develop the skills of critical viewing and reading, developing an understanding of psychological imagery, subliminal appeals, multiple musical appeals, pseudo–logical persuasion and many other propaganda techniques"; *visual art* by Art in Three Dimensions: "Typical areas of study may include sculpture, jewelry, ceramics, furniture making, boat building and architecture"; and the *library* by Research Skills, which will "introduce students to intermediate and advanced research for both college preparation and life skills. Lessons will include ... DIALOG and boolean searching, introduction to the Library of Congress system, use of government documents ... "

Yellow buses filled with athletes excused from some part or all of a school day are a common sight on American streets and highways. The Academy's daily bulletins are replete year-round with "please excuse" messages for its bus-riding student athletes. However, Academy students also fly cross country to events of certain prestige and probable scholastic opportunity paid for by the Academy. In February, some students traveled to a speech tournament at the University of California, Berkeley, and others to a debate tournament at Harvard; in March, students attended the Columbia Press Association Convention at Columbia University in New York City; in May, some students participated in the National Science Olympics in Auburn, Alabama, and others in the Catholic National Speech Tournament in Washington, DC. In addition, Academy students could choose: in September to begin a semester-long evening seminar on the Maya, 7:00–8:30 p.m. offered by two teachers; in October, to visit the exhibit the librarians prepared in recognition of Banned Books Week; in March, to go to Paris for 2 weeks to study French; in April, to learn at an all-day seminar devoted to Islamic history; and in May, to watch a puppet show in Spanish performed outside the library by a troupe of six persons from Mexico.

Of equivalent importance to the breadth of concrete learning opportunities for students are the secure and stable financial circumstances that afford teachers a most felicitous state of mind:

Affluence is a real liberating situation: You can buy books. Not all students here are affluent, but there are funds for those who aren't able to buy books. You also have the freedom to ask students to do things like the poetry project. Part of this project is to attend two poetry readings in the city. It [affluence] frees them to explore new possibilities.

This English teacher is in the enviable position of being able to implement what she can imagine is worth doing. In the same vein, another English teacher delights at her ability to "do what I want in my classes, and I've done exciting things. I can do so much experimentation in my classes." "So," I ask her, "it's not just what money will allow?" She answers, "It's more like what intellectual freedom will allow." The point of the facilitating potential of money and a climate of curricular exploration is stated by yet another teacher: "Once you have proven your own interest or expertise or whatever you call it, our wealth allows that to flourish, rather than to be stifled."

The habit of curricular exploration is developed and sustained in a climate created by sufficient material means and administrative support. Both are liberating conditions. Together they engender a force of well-grounded optimism, of justifiably high expectation, of admirable achievement. Taken together, they create a yeasty milieu for teaching and learning. Teacher openness to innovation plays out under securely reinforcing circumstances at the Academy. It is not an attribute of just the particularly bold or particularly energetic teacher; it is a functional attribute for even the most ordinary Academy teacher.

Parents

Much is written about the importance of parents as allies in the successful education of their children. Parental support is a necessary condition for schools to be at their best. Finding ways to achieve parental involvement is often a considerable challenge, particularly in the case of adolescent children. Parents somehow learn to think that it is ok to leave schooling to teachers when their children get older.

Nonetheless, say teachers, Academy parents affect their children's school conduct by the pressure they create for getting high grades and for admission to prestigious colleges and universities. Many students come from homes that provide, often insist upon, out-of-school lessons, so that students may reach school already adept at some form of artistic or athletic expression. As persons of accomplishment themselves, parents are likely to provide the means for their children to become persons of accomplishment, apart from whatever occurs at school.

Students, accordingly, come from a home climate that is anything but indifferent to achievement, academic and otherwise. Moreover, if parents are displeased with some school occurrence, they are very likely to call. As a department chair said, "They will call. They will call me at home, they will call me at night, they will call, oh yes! If they are not happy, I expect them to call. They pay $6,000 bucks. 'I'm paying $6000 for my son to have a crummy teacher?' I've had that thrown at me." "What I tell new faculty," says an experienced teacher, "is that parents have high expectations. They're hard and their children are hard on teachers."

Students

Indicators of student quality are perceptible in a variety of forms, some contained in the statistics of achievement, some in graffiti, some in the observations of teachers and the students themselves. In their teachers' judgments, students overall "range from just slightly above average to off the charts." The full range gets its fair share of Academy resources; the achievements of those who cluster at the top merit public display.

By the time my year at Edgewood Academy was complete, the boys' basketball team had won its fourth straight statewide championship; the boys' swimming team had won the state championship; girls' swimming and girls' track teams won second place in the state; an Academy girl and boy had won their respective state singles tennis championships; and a girl won the state's golf title. Academy individuals and teams are accustomed to winning in the athletic domain. They acquire experience in standing out, in being noticed, admired, even envied and resented by the much less well-equipped public and nonpublic schools with whom they compete.

Without demeaning the contribution of teachers to student success, I would emphasize the significance of peers for student development. While parents create one climate within their homes and teachers another within their classrooms, students shape a third that contributes to how individual students will respond to that of their parents and teachers. As models, norm setters, and definers of what is cool, students are a central factor in the interactions that create acceptable options.

For example, female volleyball players can learn what behavior is acceptable when they have time on their hands at a tournament. The coach describes the scene at an eight-team tournament: "Here are these girls from other teams. They're combing their hair, they're in the bleachers, they're eating or reading *Seventeen* magazine. My girls were under the bleachers doing their homework between games." Students can learn from fellow students about the unlimited applications of irony from reading the graffiti on their bathroom stalls. "'Shut up, you moron, or I'll kill you,' he hinted," and they can learn about alternative values and indignation:

The thing is people freak out about tests. All of a sudden I realized, you know, you learn about something. You'll say something, like, there's some kid who died in El Salvador and no one even knew his name. They cut his tongue out, and, you know, everyday this happens, and what the hell are you doing putting so much passion and prayer into a test. On the front page of the newspaper I was recycling there were these girls on a basketball team. They were praying and I'm, like, "What the hell are you praying for a damn basketball game when the entire world is in turmoil?"

Students praise other students for their intellectual prowess. In classes where discussion is dominant, they can claim to have received a noteworthy contribution to their own learning from peers. Though not necessarily typical, the acknowledgements of a senior student impressed me:

Last year's AP [advanced placement] history class changed me from an intellectual child to an intellectual adult. It was, I think, the intensity of the class; the discussions we had were just so amazing. I had to make myself figure out how to communicate with these people who were on a higher level than I was. It meant I had to work twice as hard as they did, but it paid off.

A mother, reflecting on her now-graduated son's experience at the Academy, speaks of a student who might have set a standard in AP history that the previous student could feel moved to emulate.

I asked my son why he was so happy there. He said, "Well, it was the first time in my life that it was all right to be smart with my peers. It was that way all the way through. If I did well on something, they were happy for me."

When parents consider what the Academy is able to offer their children, they may not focus on the quality of the student company their children keep, but they can not be impervious to the fact that their children are in the company of peers who have hurdled the same admissions barriers. Students will not be alone in almost whatever personal form and level of intellectual, athletic, and artistic singularity they bring to the Academy setting.

Teachers

Indicators of teacher quality take a variety of forms. To begin with, just as the student selection process inclines toward recruiting students who are above average in achievement and ability, the teacher selection process inclines similarly. In the view of an Academy administrator: "While teachers and administrators complain about other teachers, everyone here is competent. There may be some that are not doing the job as well as they could or should, but all the teachers here are competent."

This judgment is confirmed, at least to my satisfaction, in many ways. Consider the words of two first-year teachers: "What I said [when I got hired] was that I have sort of made some sort of grade to be in a place that upholds very strong educational values. I made that grade, like making it to the Olympic trials. Just getting there is a major accomplishment." Her counterpart in another academic department affirms this outlook when she says, "You have to live up to the institution." I take this observation seriously. How many teachers at how many schools would be apt to say approvingly that their school has standards that they aspire "to live up to," that their school's standards are inspiring. Aspiring teachers and inspiring standards strike me as hallmarks of a reputable school.

Students, moreover, learn from the models, achievements, and aspirations and attitudes their teachers embody. Here is the picture of Academy faculty achievement that derives from external affirmation:

- Teacher receives $3,500 as Sci-Math Fellow to spend 6 weeks in a study that links science and the humanities. One hundred such awards are made nationally.
- Teacher receives the Eleanor Roosevelt Award of the American Association of University Women.
- Teacher wins the state's foreign language outstanding teacher of the year award.
- Teacher, one of three in the state, wins the Presidential Award for Excellence in Science and Mathematics.
- Teacher is named Klingenstein Summer Institute Master Teacher of English at Teachers College, Columbia.
- Teacher is awarded a 6-week grant by the National Endowment of the Humanities to study Women in Literature at Great Barrington, Massachusetts.
- Teacher is invited to participate in the Woodrow Wilson Summer Institute on the History of Chemistry.

These honors span almost the entire range of Academy teaching departments. They are the ones announced during my year of study; it was not an unusual year.

Other indicators of teacher quality are discernible in teacher attitudes.[5] One teacher makes the common distinction between teaching-as-calling and as occupation, saying that it is teaching-as-calling that impresses him about the educators attracted to independent schools. Another notes that teaching is "very exciting" to her, that it "is wonderful and I love doing it" and that her philosophy

---

[5]What follows is based on multisession interviews with teachers conducted over a period of many months, which methodological note I add by way of saying, "I trust what the teachers told me." I heard enough of a discordant nature to verify that they were not bent simply on praising their school. True, teacher self-characterizations may be overly modest or overblown, but I saw the persons I quote at work in their classrooms and offices. I believe what they say.

is "you have to take risks. You will never experience passion if you stay in the middle of the road. It doesn't go there," and neither does she. She bristles with energy and devotion when she teaches. And a third comments generally about his satisfaction at being an Academy educator: "I am flattered that I am part of this school. I continue to be flattered constantly that I am considered to be a useful part of this school."

Usually, it is hard to extract superlatives about teachers from students, but Academy students have not learned to be stinting in their praise. I interviewed a senior boy just short of graduation. He prides himself on being on top of things happening at school; he always thought he knew what was being done that required student resistance or protest because students had not been consulted or because earlier understandings were being violated. I asked what, if anything, he'd probably remember about his years at the Academy. Sounding as if he thought he was being at least moderately condemning, he conceded that he'd find memorable no more than fifteen different classes he had taken, and, well, some number of both student and teachers. "Many teachers?" Certainly no more than two hands. I'd say a little over one. The really good teachers I could probably sit down with one hand, yeah. The ones I will probably remember well, probably two hands."

Many things teachers do are suggestive of their talents and commitment to student success. One such thing relates to time. How much time outside of class, during or after the school day, will teachers give to their students and how unbegrudging is their giving? Academy educators, in their roles as teachers, counselors, coaches, administrators, mentors, colleagues, and committee members, lead very busy lives. Academy educators are married, have children and parents of their own, and personal lives that they value. Thus, time given to their students is time not spent elsewhere. "In a 2-week period," recalls a student,

> I must have brought in [to his English teacher] four different papers, like essays for schools [he is a senior applying for admission to colleges and universities that require an essay], along with essays for his class. I must have been in to see him six times out of 10 days. And he went over every single one of them, and gave me advice on every single one of them. Without a blink of an eye he is willing to do that.

Incredulous at this degree of generosity, I ask the student about the normality of such teacher behavior. "This is pretty normal," he replies. "Nine out of ten teachers will do this." I cannot confirm this estimation. Since it squares with much else that I learned, I present it as an important indicator of teacher quality.

Another more general perspective on teacher quality is available from a student who reflects on what he thinks the Academy is trying to accomplish.

Well, probably not only textbook stuff. The ability to know who you are, by the time you graduate, to know what your strengths are, what your weaknesses are—I think they really want that. The ability to interpret facts, events, issues, the ability to learn from them on your own, to make analogies and metaphors … probably to be able to write … to communicate, to think rationally, to be, I guess, an enlightened person—I think that, in their minds, is important.

As for the student himself, he thought that "just in the past 2 years I've been really taught how to think on my own." From what I observed, the student is accurate on all counts, not least on his first point regarding teacher awareness of student strengths and weaknesses.

When parents criticize their child's school, is the "problem" in the school, the child, the parent, or some combination of these three? Similarly, when parents praise a school, what is going on? Some parents fault a particular teacher, citing incompetence, insensitivity, or both. Moreover, and unsurprisingly, students undergoing the same classroom experience do not necessarily experience it similarly. Take the required, senior-level class in humanities, each section taught by a pair of teachers, the teachers drawn from the departments of mathematics, science, English, and history. I heard many students gripe at their I'm-getting-nowhere sense of this required class. To the contrary, a mother reports her reactions to this class:

> Once at dinner we were discussing a really hot topic and I asked Sam [her son] what he thought. He said, "I just don't know what I think any more since I took humanities." I would have paid the $6,000 just for that. What that means is that it shook him up so he has to re-evaluate what he has always thought.

Neither all students nor all parents would value such shaking up.

Similarly, students are neither equally available for the learning that is possible in any given subject, nor available in general to benefit from what a school overall is offering. An Academy father reports about his son that "I'm seeing somebody who has incredible teachers, who is just having worlds and worlds open up for him, and getting an education that 20 years ago was not available until you got to junior and senior year in college." His son is lucky, fortunate to be attending a school whose teachers are potentially world openers, a school where such opening is not a chance event or the fortuitous outcome of some small subset of teachers, who, if they left, would take the outcome away with them.

I close this section on A Place of Quality with two internal indicators of quality. Each speaks to the Academy's merit in a different way.

A dearth of time defeats much of value, often before any effort, say, for school reform or classroom innovation, is undertaken. Next to money, it is the greatest shortage of essential teacher resources. Of course, money and time are correlated. At the Academy, the correlation is in the right direction, as noted in the pleasure of a teacher who is thinking about her former life as a public school teacher:

> Out there, I see teachers [her former colleagues] putting in 1,000 percent of their effort. They'll teach five out of six classes. They have a limited prep period. There is no time for kids to come in for tutoring. You just don't have the contact with kids there that you have here. You don't have the time to write curriculum, and you don't have the time for professional growth that this school offers.

Time for students, curriculum development, professional growth—these are truly critical aspects of a teacher's life. Because money can be counted on to be available, time can, too. What is begun can be finished; what is imagined can be implemented. As this teacher compares her past and present life as an educator, she sounds as if she is luxuriating, but time for becoming and being a sound educator is by no means a luxury.

What else does money buy at the Academy? It buys materials and space, the stuff that transforms ideas into the particulars of practice. It buys the optimism that Academy educators reveled in; their dreams, if well-conceived, were within their grasp. It buys smaller class size, which at least enables teachers to give more time to each student, and also to feel less pressure of the type that leads to burnout. And, possibly, it "buys" the choice of educators from an expanded cadre of candidates, one that might include persons formerly unwilling to make the financial sacrifices that school systems everywhere take for granted.

That time is appreciated by Academy faculty is absolutely clear in the strong but hyperbolic language of the teacher who affirmed that "the greatest blessing that the Academy ever had was the fact that it was wealthy enough to ensure that there always was enough time."

I conclude with one last general indicator of quality, a clearly subjective one that would not have been revealed by any ordinary test of achievement that a school or agency would normally administer. Though tests currently administered may have their value, they would not uncover what I believe any school would value knowing about itself. I asked a student to consider that if he had gone to some other school, would he be pretty much the same person he is today. It was near the end of the school year, by which time I felt confident to ask questions of an abstractness that had not previously occurred to me to ask. The student's answer:

> My parents have given me an incredible amount, but I still wouldn't have—this is so speculative—I really don't know if I would have the same knowledge of myself as I do here. I think if I was put in another school, I would still be kind of searching for something. I've kind of thought of this as me being some huge jig-

saw puzzle and I just acquired the last, not the last piece, not in the least the last piece, but one very important, intricate piece to this puzzle of me that I don't think I would have found somewhere else.

What we can infer with confidence from this young man's self-analysis is that he is pleased with his Academy education. What we cannot know is the warrant for what he acknowledges is speculative, but, then, there is no research model available that could establish such warrant. The uncommon nature of the student's acclaim, coupled with my sense of his reputability, inclines me to affirm that it reflects most positively on the Academy's educative accomplishments.

The intent of this chapter, beyond identifying Edgewood Academy as an independent school and describing it in very general terms, has been to clarify its mission of excellence and to verify it as a place of excellence realized. Thereby do I acknowledge both what I believe is demonstrably true but also where one major strand of my own subjectivity lies—my "Dazzled-I": Never before had I seen or experienced any school like it. I felt I was in an educational wonderland. Soon after I arrived, I wished that my own children had been able to attend such a school; in time, I wished that I had, as well.

3

Judgments for Excellence

Teacher (T): The students' own excellence makes the teachers strive to be better. I really do believe that.

AP: But you come in as strivers, I would think. You are selected because you look like you've been a striver.

T: Yes, you've been an achiever.

AP: So, you're picked in the same way the kids are picked.

T: That's right. It's just this crazy environment where everybody is wonderful and no matter what you do, it's not wonderful enough because there is somebody else doing something just as wonderful. And then we are all evaluated. All the wonderful are evaluating the wonderful. Not everyone, but too many of us are extrinsically motivated. So your evaluation becomes a great importance. I guess that plays into a kind of neurotic behavior, sort of no matter what you do, it's never enough. It's not a good situation and yet, you know, it's the best job in town.[1]

---

[1]This is not hyperbole. Edgewood Academy is in an educational and financial class by itself in the entire state. There are other independent schools nearby and elsewhere that satisfy other educational tastes and pocketbooks. Unlike independent schools in larger cities and states, the Academy has no serious competition.

Given that nonpublic schools are schools of choice, and choice obviously necessitates judgment, it seems most appropriate to continue my depiction of Edgewood Academy with a discussion of several of its major occasions for judgment making. They involve the selection of students and teachers, and also the evaluation and growth of teachers. In large part, a school is known by the quality of its judgments. An estimation of quality includes the soundness of the process a school devises for the judgments it makes, the capacity of the people it chooses to conduct the process, and the faithfulness of these people to the principles underlying the process.

SELECTING STUDENTS

> I wrote a real good paragraph, but I was terrified that I was doomed to go to public school for the rest of my life.
>
> *—Academy applicant*

> If people don't get into here it is a bigger deal to them than if they don't get into Harvard. I have been told that time and time again.
>
> *—Academy administrator*

The Academy's Director of Admissions receives some inquiries from parents whose children are not yet born and more from parents whose children are 18 months to 3-years old. The aspirants for Academy advantage are zealous. For example, in 1991–1992, the school received 1,596 inquiries about admission; the school accepted 29% of the 830 students who actually applied. Of those accepted, 82% entered the next fall, most of them at the sixth grade level, but some at the upper grades where there were a few openings. In the course of the same year, there was an attrition rate of 3.7%; given that four of the students who left did so because their family moved away, the attrition rate declines to 2.6%.

One point of these statistics is to affirm that the school and the students it selects enjoy sufficient mutual satisfaction so that most of those who do enroll stay there. Another point, and one that goes to the heart of such private schools, is the matter of selectivity: Edgewood Academy is such an appealing place that many students and their parents strongly desire admission, which means that the school can be selective. Although as a nonboarding school its pool of applicants is local and thus narrower than that of the elite boarding schools of the East, it nonetheless has the basis for being selective. Table 3.1 provides a picture of interest in Academy admission; the data, although basically reassuring, indicates a fairly steady decline in actual applications.

By chance, the first time I made an extended visit to the school, the next fall's admission deliberations were underway. I was eager to observe the committee at work, but unsure how my request to view what I thought might be considered a sensitive matter would be received. I was given permission, and thus received an early indication that I would have full access to the school's activities and deliberations.

The committee began its meeting after school and continued its work through dinnertime and thereafter. Teachers were called on to work without extra compensation long after class work was done. But this was not the post-school day work of coaches, drama teachers, and club sponsors. It was everyone's work of school governance, broadly considered to include matters such as admissions or curriculum development. Box dinners were duly delivered, as I learned would always be true for school work conducted through any meal time; then, 1 hour of talk followed another, until I grew tired and left long before this tireless committee went home for the night. I was impressed by the devotion that kept this group in focus, its workload immense, the stakes high both for the aspiring students and the school. I was also impressed by the group's commitment to being thorough and fair in its choices. Appreciating that student selection is a distinguishing aspect of such schools, I made a mental note to return to this process when I came for my full year of fieldwork, believing that it would instruct me about the school in an important way.

During that year, over the course of several consecutive days spread across the end of March and the beginning of April, a committee composed of teachers, middle-level administrators, the director of financial aid, and the director of admissions met in a room set aside for meetings. The Director of Admissions, a full-time, year-round position, led the proceedings. All present had received the large packet of information required for each applicant. I will elaborate on the

TABLE 3.1
Edgewood Academy Admissions Data 1993–1994 Through 1997–1998*

	1994	1995	1996	1997	1998
Inquiries	1,750	1,801	1,803	1,681	1,503
Applications	865	746	680	702	636
Accepted	212	214	224	213	234
Percent Accepted	25	29	33	30	37
Enrolled	179	182	189	194	193

*These data refer to students applying to Grades 6 to 12.

contents of this packet in order to demonstrate how substantial a data set the Academy insisted on as the basis for its decision making. We learn from all this what it means to be a "select" school.

From all indications during the several days of discussion, the committee members had done their homework; they had perused the packet, made their summary estimations on a scale of 1 to 6, and came prepared to deliberate with their fellows. Their collective judgments would lead applicants to acceptance, to rejection, or to a wait list. Their rankings were recorded on what looked like an easel, but was, in fact, a Canon Board Copier, a device that can automatically print whatever is written on its large writing surface.

Underlying each member's ranking was information from the student's application form, some of it demographic, but more of it directly germane to the committee's judgment making. For example, the students had to list both their in-school and out-of-school activities. Activities figured notably in the distinctions committee members would make, in the belief that each reveals something consequential about a person. The admission packet also contained a list of dates for when applicants could come to the Academy campus to take a mathematics test and provide a writing sample. On this same occasion, applicants toured the campus while their parents attended a separate information session. Parents received a school-records release form that, when signed, would authorize the Academy to obtain a copy of their child's official school record. This provided the Academy with a student's grades, an essential piece of information.

Another part of the applicant packet contained two recommendation forms, one for the student's English teacher, another for the mathematics teacher; the perspective of teachers of other subject matter was not deemed important. The English and mathematics teachers were invited to make an assessment of the applicant's academic merits on a 6-point scale, ranging from poor to "one of the top few encountered in my career." The specifics of their assessment included ranking students on ability, motivation, curiosity, growth potential, academic creativity, and academic independence. On another 6-point scale, each teacher also was invited to rate student character as it relates to leadership, self-confidence, warmth of personality, sense of humor, energy, maturity, reaction to criticism, respect accorded by faculty, and respect accorded by peers. In addition to these ratings, the recommending teachers were asked to list adjectives that describe the students academically and personally, to discuss areas of needed improvement, and to conclude by rating the student, again on a 6-point scale, in regard to academic promise, personal promise, and, finally, overall.

Committee members infused their considerations of each student's suitability for admission with perspectives and weightings that represented their own particular values; this was not a by-the-numbers deliberation. At the extremes, decisions came easily. Those applicants who garnered a string of sixes invited little to no discussion. They were admitted. Those who garnered threes or lower were not. Those who fell in between—the fours and the fives—challenged the committee members, and it was to them that the members devoted their greatest energy, looking for those indicators that most convincingly and fairly discriminated among the applicants. How to distinguish between what student attributes and scores signaled the basis for making a sound or unsound choice preoccupied the committee. One of the members cautioned that it was not the school's practice "to get bad kids out. Once in, they stay in unless they are outrageous. So, we need to be tough." I listened carefully to learn what it might mean "to be tough."

Student scores on the mathematics test often were weighted so heavily that a low score, notwithstanding positive impressions from other admission material, would disqualify. A low score indicated that a student could not do mathematics at an Academy level of acceptability. When, however, this lockstep action disqualified minority candidates, whose admission in general was a high priority, then mathematics test scores came in for some reconsideration: "I say, if she's [otherwise] gifted, maybe she'll blossom here. We go so heavy on the math, but what about the other qualities? If they're creative people, do they need to be so good in math? I can't eliminate kids just because of math." This leads to an on-the-one-hand other-hand discussion of what anguish students face at the Academy if they are not good in mathematics, and, conversely, how fine students are excluded when the importance of mathematics as an admission criterion is overemphasized.

Discussing minority students, which included mostly Mexican Americans (or Hispanics, as termed by the state), African Americans, and, to a lesser extent, Native Americans, added an edge to the deliberations. All members were fully apprised of the school's commitment to diversity, the shorthand label for attracting and admitting students from underrepresented minority groups. I never heard anyone resist this policy. When, however, the minority student's test scores or grades were not readily reassuring, and "other factors" of a mitigating sort were introduced in order to make a case for admission, then uncertainty, if not incredulity, would become apparent.

On the one hand, the Hispanic students most often were poor and their families may have had no tradition of success in schools. These parents and children did not easily entertain the idea of being "Academy material"; it seemed like a presumptuous leap. On the other, Academy educators made vigorous efforts to overcome this reluctance and to promulgate the notion that the Academy was, indeed, a most thinkable alternative to the public schools if a child had given evidence of academic merit of a comparatively high order. If, when emboldened, families and students entered the elaborate admission process and met with failure when they expected success, this outcome could undermine the school's emboldening efforts. Such outcomes were inevitable; seeking admission to such a selective institution entails rejection. Given all this, the committee strained to be fair, to see merit where, at first, they did not; to reconsider cases originally assessed late at night when they admitted to feeling tired; and to weigh mitigating circumstances that could construe less-than-reassuring student scores within a context that softened their impact. As an academically demanding institution, the Academy would not knowingly admit anyone whose record suggested a higher risk of failure than success. But it would always take more than the committee could ever know about any of the applicants to be sure how actually handicapping any one or set of their presumed handicaps would prove to be.

I learned about the difficulties of making judgments to accept or reject when the minority student was not located in a category of mostly fives and sixes. In the course of asking a committee member what one knew from a student's grades, he said that it tells us about an applicant's study skills and ability, and he would not reject the worth of such information. But thinking of the minority applicant, he saw a problem with who, possibly, is eliminated: "the person who has gone from a C to a B and is on the way up and cannot fight the straight A students. He has a mindset [that holds him back]. The starting gate was just different." Determining what to make of different starting gates requires Solomonic wisdom. The committee struggled to be wise.

So, for example, different committee members said of different applicants: "He has all As, but immaturity is written all over the place." "Her social life is out of control, though she has high math and writing scores." "He does not have one friend," to which someone retorts, but "I think it's unfair to rule out kids who are loners." "That kid is sneaky and lazy. We should reject him even though he has very high scores." "I don't need another student who complains about homework. You should see what a moody student does to a class." The group identifies several categories of nonacademic attributes—social life, character, and temperament—that they apply in their judgment to include or exclude.

The ambiguous assessment of "smart with poor test scores" can be made acceptable by a teacher's recommendation. So it is with a student who got straight As in mathematics for 5 years, but scored average on the Academy's mathematics test. A strong letter from the grade school mathematics teacher ruled this student in. "Lazy" is the appellation of another applicant's teacher. "Smart but lazy can rule you out," someone says. "This kid cries a lot and misses school a lot. How could he survive here?" "She had good recommendations that say she goes the extra mile." Going an "extra mile" adds a big plus to any applicant's case. It suggests "good character," a quality that the Academy appreciates and will take seriously for discriminating among students otherwise deemed equal. Over and over, the group would settle on low character ratings as the basis for rejection. "He's got a 3½ [out of 6] on his character. I can deny him. That character thing jumps out at you." The 3½ was the applicant's average score on character, derived from the ratings each committee member gave this student. For a moment, the group would reflect on the judgment of whether the "character thing" also jumped at them, since the otherwise reaffirming data of grades and test scores were pointing to acceptance. Indeed, the character thing presented a tough obstacle to overcome, but it could be overcome by the consideration that, for example, the student "is a female chess player and I'm going to change my ranking" or "I like this student because his parents are a dishwasher and a maid. That's diversity."

Context increasingly becomes a factor as the group warms to the arduous task of making distinctions about those tough cases of fours and fives. The more the group needs to make distinctions, the more it finds the bases for making them, defining what personal attributes or circumstances should make a difference.

As the committee's deliberations wind down, a very tired group yearns for its work to be over, but the admissions procedure is too important to rush. It is the conduit to their classrooms and lunchrooms and gymnasia for years to come; moreover, each admitted student serves as an advertisement to the community beyond the Academy, a positive or negative living emblem of what the school signifies.

I marvel that the committee can reach consensus on whom to accept, reject, or place on the waiting list, given the variable weighting the members give to this or that criterion. The committee includes those who attend primarily to grades, who believe that this indicator of accomplishment is the surest measure of an applicant's capacity for academic success and willingness to pursue it. Though no one present disputes the salience of this measure, when it is put alongside other facts, it assumes different degrees of centrality. For example, one member recalled afterward that "on our recommendation forms is one little line that says, 'concern for others.' I could not believe how much we were scrutinizing that one piece [of information]." They achieve some reconciling of their variable weightings when they make explicit why they made the rankings as they did. Thus, when a student has received a set of 5s and one 4, the person marking 4 is invited to explain why; similar explanations are invited for the single high ranking. In this way, the rest of the group attains access to perspectives that did not occur to them. This is part of the group's continuing process of self-education. In the unfolding articulations, individuals learn about their own minds, and that of the other committee members.

Given the number and quality of students aspiring to enter Edgewood Academy, the school has to choose whom it believes belongs there. Independent schools can fashion an institutional mission, and then set about attracting students who appear to be congruent with that mission. Thus, when the admission committee emphasized an applicant's character, it was expressing every educator's interest in students who are decent, motivated, caring, and honest. By means of its elaborate judgment process, the committee could fairly well ascertain that its chosen students were: academically proficient, motivated to succeed, could do well under pressure (as in being interviewed and tested in new, unfamiliar circumstances), and were strivers, achievers, and competitors. Teachers agreed that this was the type of student who entered and stayed in the Academy, one who was prepared to capitalize on the educationally privileging experience that an Academy education afforded.

SELECTING EDUCATORS

T: This fellow, you can see from his sheet there, at 1:12 today he will be demonstration teaching in an AP History class. It's up to him to take the class and introduce himself and run it for the period.

AP: He knew about this and the topic in advance?

T: Yes, it's "democracy in America." You know, a piece of cake.

(Discussion with department chair)

AP: This is serious business [I say to a department chair about hiring a new teacher].

T: Oh, hell, It's one of the most important things I do here, I think. Because, after all, when you get right down to brass nails, you know, it is self-evident that this school, with all of its wonderful bricks and mortar and fancy facilities, is really, in the end, only going to be as good as the faculty and students who fill it.

(Discussion with department chair)

The recruitment of Academy students is a local matter; students must live within commuting distance because the school has no boarding facilities. Though there has been talk about the opening of boarding facilities in order to attract the very best students from anywhere in the world, this idea is not yet of high priority in the school's development plans. Unlike students, Academy educators may come from anywhere in the nation, for the Academy has both the reputation to attract teachers from wherever they are currently working and the financial means to fly them in for several days of mutual inspection.

I did not chance to sit with a committee deliberating over which teacher to hire of the several who had come hoping to be chosen for a vacant position. I did, however, listen to key persons in the hiring process, the department chairs, as they expanded on what they look for in a teacher. Their "looking" occurs when they examine a candidate's resumé, conduct telephone conversations prior to the campus visit, and, last, during the campus visit, when they are with the candidate, who spends most of 2 days being listened to and seen. The scrutiny is careful, intense, and searching, certainly matching in seriousness the looking done by the student selection committee.

Department chairs do not follow a script that lays out what attributes and achievements an Academy teacher should possess. They follow their strongly personal sense of who would be a good teacher in their department. So it is that the English department chair can speak of salivating when he sees from a candidate's papers that he has "a liberal arts degree from a selective school and a multiplicity of involvements beyond the classroom." This is what strongly appeals to him. Evidence of such a background is in the candidate's application. Should this candidate make the paper cut and come to the Academy for a visit, the chair looks for "warmth, compatibility, congeniality, and especially flexibility." In the course of interviewing the candidate, the chair is likely to ask, "What was your family life like? Describe your most memorable and influential teacher. What materials have you found to be especially effective with one group of students or another?"

The mathematics chair would not necessarily reject any of his English colleague's priorities, but he states his case differently. Given his view of teaching mathematics, he favors candidates who see their subject as an art form, as creative play. For him, academic degrees convey limited information; sitting down with that person is what counts, for then you can see if "that person can appeal to our students, and if they can deal with our students and our issues." He wants to hear how they deal with mistakes they make while teaching, and if they see opportunity in something that developed in class that was in no way part of their plan for that day's work. He says, "I want somebody who is going to be willing to go out on a bit of a limb with students."

When the chairs say nothing about their teacher candidates needing a teaching certificate, I ask them about it. One chair states with finality that he desires advanced work in subject matter, not in education, and another that if the teacher is brand new or inexperienced, then, but only then, is practice teaching valuable. Experienced teachers, it is thought, have already overcome the problems of getting started in their classroom, and therefore do not need either the courses or the practice that accompany a teaching certificate. Department chairs are most attracted to a candidate's subject matter background, preferring relevant degrees up through the master's. Academy teachers whose prior jobs were in public schools more typically have taken the conventional educational route to the classroom, but the department chairs dismiss education courses as too theoretical and having no clear basis for classroom success, as they view it. One department chair acknowledged the utility of a practical course in pedagogy that he had taken. It was "less of theory and more of practice. A course like that is certainly worthwhile," he said, "as opposed to a course in school and community."

Some of the Academy's best educators, as I viewed them, came up through the ranks of teacher education and public schools; others, equally outstanding, had not. Some of those who had done so scorned their teacher education experience, together with what they viewed as their stultifying experiences in public schools. They thought they had found themselves as educators in the freedom of the independent school. In the end, I could collect strong feelings, even convictions, but, certainly, nothing amounting to evidence that there was a sure route to successful pedagogical practice, let alone consensus about what constitutes success. It is worth exploring what difference teacher training makes, just as it is worth noting that many teachers who work in schools that do not require teacher certification for employment are models of excellence.

The path to finding the candidates for Academy job openings takes various forms. Head hunters who specialize in independent school jobs make the connection between candidates and job openings, much as they do in any employment field, but applicants literally line up for recruitment to Academy employment. Each year, the headmaster receives over 1,000 unsolicited letters of inquiry. These are sent not in response to a known vacancy, but as an uninvited expression of interest in working at the Academy; the inquirers want their names to be kept on file in the event that a job opens up. In fact, department chairs do save these files, taking note of who looks special on paper and can be contacted when a vacancy opens. Says one chair, "I have my own file, about a foot thick, of letters of inquiry, resumés, letters of recommendation, dossiers from university placement offices." In addition, the chairs may advertise their open positions in appropriate journals, presenting a job description and a salary level that has been negotiated with the headmaster. For a recent position in the history department, the chair received about 250 applications and, thus, the responsibility of sifting through a mound of aspirations.

Some chairs do all the sorting themselves; others enlist their faculty. By one means or another, the sorting is accomplished and a favored few are invited to the campus, where the process of judgment making continues. The Academy's reputation precedes an applicant's visit; the experience of the visit does nothing to diminish its reputation. The occasion of a search, with its flood of applicants, reminds current Academy teachers and administrators of their good fortune in being an Academy educator. To be among the chosen is heady, no matter the field.

To be among the few chosen to make the 2-day, all expenses paid visit to the Academy also is heady. Visiting candidates may attend a breakfast reception in the library with department teachers before going off to observe different classrooms; they may attend a department dinner with perhaps no more than eight other people, so that the dinner talk can be focused on learning about the candidate, and the candidate learning about the department and the school. Departments want all their faculty members to meet the candidate and provide feedback to the department chair. Perhaps the most challenging expectation for a candidate is teaching an actual class. Sometimes, this performance is sharply convincing of the candidate's merit: "The woman we hired sat in Bill's class one day and then taught it the next day. I had never seen anyone do that kind of a job. I couldn't do it; she had all of us in awe." The "all of us" is the department chair and several other senior faculty who watched the newcomer perform and whose assessment would be part of the thrust to hire or not. The woman was hired.

Other candidates, less fortunate, look good on paper, sound convincing over the course of several telephone calls, but seen up close they bomb: "You know, it was fundamental points of intellect and personality, even character. He was terribly fawning, whining, you know, obsequious. Oh, it was dreadful. He was one of those people who wanted the job so desperately that he just made a fool of himself. No one should want a job that bad."

Department chairs collect all the data they can, using student and faculty judgments to reach a conclusion that is then brought to "the boss," the headmaster. One chair says, "In my first 2 or 3 years as chair, I would meet with Mr. Compton and present my personal assessment and my read of what the departmental consensus is, if any. After a while, when our views coincided so closely, he said, 'You make a judgment, it's your call. If you want to hire him, hire him.'"

I asked several recently hired teachers to recall the process of making contact with the Academy and getting hired: "I heard there was an opening at the Academy, and I contacted them. I was going to the National Association of Independent Schools conference because there's a hiring fair there, the meat market for teachers." He found the Academy's table that had been set up for meeting interested candidates, met several of the department chairs in attendance there, and left. He knew the Academy was interested in him because he had an Ivy League education and had already taught at a prominent eastern boarding school. "I am what they create, right? So that makes me a marketable commodity."

Another new teacher began her contact with a head hunter, who arranged an interview with Mr. Compton. She remembers that he described the students' capabilities, the size of the school's endowment, and its commitment to diversity.

"He asked me to put modesty aside and elaborate on what I do best. I told him that I felt I had come into my own as a teacher, I had developed some style, and I wanted to grow and had room to grow. This wasn't happening at my former school. In response, he talked a lot about the Academy's evaluation system and its mentoring. I told him I craved evaluation because I had had none. I knew we connected at this first meeting."

A third new teacher first met Mr. Compton in New York, where he happened to be for a visit. The teacher already had had some phone calls with the department chair, and there was some mutual interest. The meeting with Mr. Compton was persuasive. "It was a huge, positive experience. He [Compton] was tremendous—personable, warm, and open-minded, someone you could trust. In independent schools, the tradition of mistreating teachers is very strong, but I knew he was different. He told me to come out the next week for a visit." From the candidate's visit to the Academy campus, he learned that

> I liked the people I met. They seemed down-to-earth. I felt terrific by the end of the 2½ days. The afternoon of the last day the headmaster offered me the job. I was bouncing off the ceiling of the airplane on the way home. The most important thing for me, other than the physical plant and the endowment, was that I trusted the people. I felt that I wasn't taking a chance by coming across the country to this new job. I knew I would be treated well for being a good teacher.

From these three new employees, I see the importance of having the right credentials as a very strong starting point for Academy interest in a candidate, but such credentials are just a foot in the door. The second of the three, with not quite the "right" credentials, established her attractiveness by her desire for growth and evaluation. Such a candidate has a decided edge for being hired, if other things are reasonably equal. And they may well be, as it is for students who are not ranked with straight 6s in all the categories of assessment, but who otherwise look so appealing that the evaluators must take them seriously. As a much more experienced teacher with an established reputation, the third teacher was in a position to be looking critically at the Academy, and wondering whether he wanted to risk changing jobs. Trust communicated by headmaster and colleagues-to-be persuaded him that it was the right thing to do.

Teachers and department chairs conclude that the hiring process generally brings in teachers who are diamonds—the experienced teacher with a track record of excellence, or diamonds-in-the-rough—the relative newcomer who demonstrates considerable promise for becoming a diamond. As with students, the Academy invests much in the teacher-selection process, for the results also constitute a fact to be lived with for years to come. A department chair reflects on the hiring process that he had recently gone through:

I felt like I had to be at my intellectual and sort of receptive peak at all times when I was around the candidates. I had to make sure that I was presenting my department and my school correctly, plus I had to be in tune with the candidate's vibes: "Is this somebody I can work with? Is it somebody I would trust living up to my expectations and those of the department?" It was exhausting, but I also know that the person I recommend to be hired will probably have more impact on the school than anything else I do this year.

I see in the elite nonpublic schools' judgments the opportunity to forge a close fit among students, teachers, and educative purpose. Given sound judgment-making procedures, the schools need then to develop a promising pool of applicants from which to choose. The Academy's reputation provides, perhaps guarantees, such a pool of both students and teachers. The school makes every effort to overcome any limitations that might result from its choice of students and teachers being confined just to locally available candidates. The Academy means to have access to the best of all local students and to the best of all teachers from anywhere in the nation. Theirs is not a farfetched aspiration.

TEACHER EVALUATION

You know, there are very few teachers that are gross, obvious, bye-bye cases. Most of them are people who do adequate-to-good work. What is sought is really remarkable work. That's the ideal. How to achieve that is, I suppose, through this evaluative process, and through other mechanisms that we might devise, including professional development funds, which are very generous.

—Department chair

Research has finally told us what many of us suspected all along: That conventional evaluation, the kind the overwhelming majority of American teachers undergo, does not have any measurable impact on the quality of student learning. In most cases, it is a waste of time.

—Mike Schmoker (1992, p. 23)

> *AP:* There is no tenure here, so, theoretically, everybody can be replaced?
>
> *T:* Yes. Now, that said, it's not happened in my experience that anyone has been told, 'you're good, but you're not good enough,' much less, 'you're good, but there's much better out there.' The school has been more than humane about not expeditiously shooing out beached whales. The school has not been that ruthless, but I think there is the perception that at some point it could be.

(Discussion with department chair)

Mike Schmoker might be persuaded that the Academy's teacher evaluation system is far from "conventional" and not "a waste of time." Lacking evidence of any type, he would have no basis for determining whether it had "any measurable impact on the quality of learning." His interest is in the right type of outcome—"student learning," but he sets no slight task when he asks for making a connection between teacher evaluation and "measurable" student learning. The Academy has never tried to obtain such results. Assuming, however, that unwatched teachers do not perform at their best, it has constructed a thoroughly unconventional plan for insuring that its teachers are watched, watched often, and watched well. By presenting details of this plan, I intend to indicate what the Academy does to verify that it takes seriously the performance of its teachers. I do not mean to be recommending this practice, any other practice, or, for that matter, what the Academy does overall as ideal for the Academy or any other school. I most definitely mean to affirm that when the Academy privileges teacher performance, it contributes more certainly to the quality of its teachers and thus to the advantage of its students.

The present evaluation system is the product of Mr. Compton's leadership. It broadcasts growth as its primary intent, but teachers believe it has as much or more to do with judgments that will underlie salary increases and, possibly, dismissal, given the Academy's prevailing nontenure system of employment. A department chair hired soon after Compton's arrival recalls that the promulgation of his new evaluation system created widespread anxiety. "Faculty believed that the purpose of the evaluation was to conduct a general purge of Stalinesque quality, and people like myself were brought in to be the axemen." The purge has not occurred, and is not likely to occur.

When I began my year-long association with the Academy, the first planned meeting of the new school year brought together all department chairs and other administrators. At the top of the agenda for their late August, pre-school discussions was a document called Guide to Evaluation. It contained the complete text of those guidelines that direct the work of supervision for which each chair is responsible. The intent of the August meeting was to reclarify the procedure for the benefit of both the old and the newly appointed chairs.

Department chairs are perched at the apex of the evaluation process. Their teaching loads are adjusted so that they are available to guide the process, visit classrooms themselves, and prepare the report that goes to the teacher, dean, and headmaster. Evaluation is not an extra task added atop their classroom responsibility; it is a basic responsibility. It requires them to be skilled observers; to have a broad view of the range of forms effective teaching can assume; to have writing skills that incorporate what they and others have seen; to have managerial skills, so that all the people and parts of the process are coordinated in timely fashion; and to have good interpersonal skills that enable them to present the findings supportively, lucidly, and cogently. In the final analysis, the impact of what they say rests on their capacity to relate to teachers who perceive themselves as vulnerable because of what may be the effects of the assessment report on salary increases, continuing employment, and the respect their superiors afford them.

At the outset of the August discussion, the Dean for Academic and Student Affairs, the administrator ranked just below the headmaster, clarified that the document everyone had in hand was the "standard from which to depart," a point more fully elaborated in the document's preface: "No one should feel constrained by these suggestions, but rather encouraged to return to [them] to discover license for more sensible ways to administer its evaluative policies. In the spirit, then, of seeking a balance between flexibility and uniformity, we offer this guide as a starting point … "

Extending this invitation to flexibility and interpretation bespeaks of audacity. This setting forth with one hand and qualifying with the other reflects the Headmaster's confidence that order can be maintained, notwithstanding the opportunity to depart from an established standard. And it reflects trust in the good sense of those who will be the perpetrators and arbiters of the program of evaluation. It assumes that they will be responsive to the spirit of the guidelines, and that when they turn away from the letter of what is set forth, there is good warrant to do so. Being so invited shows respect for the intelligence of the chairs and belief in their commitment to doing the right thing. This is as an audacious act. It is easier to operate administratively when the spirit and letter of school policy are coterminous, when there is not authorized leeway to interpret.

The Guide to Evaluation notes that the purposes of teacher evaluation are to "increase teaching effectiveness," "encourage individual growth," "document areas of concern," and "articulate suggestions for improvement." Most striking is what the Guide says about the quantitative dimension of the teacher evaluation process: "Our current agreement is to visit a teacher six times per section [class] taught; thus a teacher of four sections might be visited a dozen times by the chair and six times by each of the two peer evaluators." This number of visits—24—is the annual total for those teachers who have not yet achieved "senior" status. Nonsenior teachers are reviewed annually, senior teachers every 4 years.

To be sure, frequency is no guarantee of quality, but the concern for quality is evident in other "suggestions" to chairs that the Guide to Evaluation contains: "as soon as the peer evaluators are agreed on, the whole team should discuss what the teacher wants observed, along with the chair's agenda"; "do not pass the final copy of the evaluation on to the Dean and the Headmaster without first discussing it with the teacher and the rest of the team"; "assume full responsibility for creating, distributing, and processing the student evaluations"; "see to it that the peer evaluators are spreading the visits out over time, and touch base often with them for early feedback." Although the chairs may implement this mammoth task of supervision in personal, idiosyncratic ways, they can not doubt that it is a most serious aspect of their job, and they do not have the prerogative to construe it otherwise.

Given the many bits of data that go into the report for each teacher evaluated, the Guide lists what the chairs should assemble "prior to writing": the results of the previous spring's student evaluations; the previous June's annual report that each teacher prepares; the chair's notes on classroom visits; the peer evaluators' notes on classroom visits; copies of tests, quizzes, handouts, course outlines, etc.; and copies of previous evaluations. The last of the many suggestions to chairs informs them that they should link "evaluation with development." When the chairs have completed their evaluation reports, they are reminded to "close by mentioning the professional development fund as a resource for promoting growth." Accordingly, just as the chairs cannot choose to underplay the importance of their role as evaluators, teachers must understand that becoming better is to be an ordinary attribute of their professional role.

To be designated as a "senior" teacher, one must have 10 years of teaching experience at the Academy, a master's degree in one's subject matter, and have demonstrated sound classroom capabilities to the satisfaction of one's department chair and the headmaster. Achieving this status, however, does not guarantee comfort with the evaluation process. For teachers bring to the process the variables of personality and temperament that tend some to comfort, others to discomfort with the evaluating observers who enter the usually closed space of their classroom. "I wanted to be evaluated," recalls one senior teacher, "but even at that it was impossible for me not to feel very vulnerable with it, you know." She confesses that any time one is evaluated there is stress, "especially for us overachievers at this school—you always want to be your best." To the contrary, a senior teacher unabashedly acknowledged, "My evaluation is like an eight-page eulogy. I could hardly read it. I feel like I'm dead, it's so filled with praise."

In one form or another, evaluation anxiety is expressed repeatedly. Teachers say: "I watched the door a little bit today, wondering if they'd come. I had an anxiety dream last night … "; "I was a little bit intimidated in the beginning … "; and "There has always been some vague element of fear … " These are the prefatory expressions of three junior teachers. In each case, anxiety notwithstanding, they go on to praise a process that on balance they find rewarding. As do older, more experienced teachers, as well:

> I had a lot to learn, and I mean it from the bottom of my heart. The way I have best learned to be a better teacher is through the evaluation process. It makes me

think about things. It makes me record things in my annual report. It makes me take assessments of myself ... My department chair is very careful, very thorough, very honest, and very gentle.

The constructive criticism that I've got came in the form of a question, which I thought was a wonderful way of presentation—'Have you thought about ... ' 'Have you tried ... ' 'What do you think about this ... ' It's a wonderful technique for having me look at another way. I never got the impression that I was doing anything wrong.

In the Academy's elaborate system of evaluation, I saw no utopian system, and no one represented it to me in such terms. What I did see was an imperfect procedure that by its scale unmistakably signals that teacher quality is extremely important and that getting better is absolutely expected. To be taken so seriously is for teachers a daunting, exhausting experience, but it is no less than the education of everyone's children merits. The school's evaluation system is consistent with Headmaster Compton's goal of excellence, as are the arrangements he has made for teacher growth.

THE MEANS FOR GROWTH

The last judgment I discuss in this chapter relates to the professional development fund. A large sum of money is set aside for the use of all faculty, ultimately at the discretion of the dean, the gatekeeper of the funds. In fact, the decision to have such a fund rests on the prior one that teacher growth is primary. It is easy to announce the importance of growth; to elevate it to an operating canon of professional conduct is another matter. An institution cannot sensibly stress the centrality of growth for teachers without providing both the means (the evaluation system) for uncovering the direction their growth should take and the resources (time and opportunity) for making their growth attainable.

The development fund is "included annually in the dean's operating budget." In the year of my study, the fund contained $200,000 for the use of about 125 faculty members, though there is no prorating principle in effect, and, thus, no sense of an individual being entitled to a particular share. The money may be used to obtain advanced degrees or for "pursuing programs of study, either at a college or university, or as independent work directly applicable to classroom or other school-related duties." Requests for study support are approved by the dean, in consultation with department chairs; no money can be used for room and board. The fund may be used to attend conferences and workshops, and also for sabbatical leaves for senior faculty after 7 full years of Academy service. The dean and the headmaster must approve such leaves; they provide full salary for one semester, or one-half salary for two.

The fund also covers the work of the inservice committee, which plans workshops and lectures for the benefit of the entire faculty:

> We talked about this idea of excellence. What are the ways that this school can bring people here, instead of just sending people out to various places? What are the most important things that we need to know to work on our teaching to keep it excellent, if it is, or to make it better? That is our charge,

explains a member of this committee. Excellence is allied to growth. What could be taken for hubris elsewhere is taken as normal at the Academy. Seeking excellence is congruent with the magnitude of the Academy's investment of resources and effort in its selection of students and faculty, and in its evaluation system and development fund. Hard work, growth, and excellence epitomize Academy life. Clearly, this triad establishes working conditions that may challenge, pressure, motivate, and intimidate its students and faculty.

In practice, teachers use the fund to do all the things that their handbook spells out, including the pursuit of activities that respond to the critiques in their evaluations. They take advantage of its munificence to enroll in colleges and universities that their own salaries would never allow; to attend subject matter conferences and meetings of independent school educators anywhere in the country; to travel abroad for crosscultural opportunities that provide knowledge and experience unavailable at home; and to seize opportunities that require a full semester or full academic year. When, for aspiring teachers, money to do is underwritten by time to do, then the best possible conditions exist for growth. A teacher illustrates how the fund operates for her:

> I'm enrolled in something called the Teacher Enhancement Program. It is a special program designed for mid-career teachers. They pull you out of class a half day on Wednesday and a full day on Thursday, and then you go all summer for several summers. You know, this school is not heavily into substitutes [meaning that a teacher is not ordinarily brought in to replace an absent teacher], so I felt really honored that they would allow me to hire a substitute teacher for the entire year that would take over for me 1½ days each week.

Academy aspirations mark it as a singular educational institution. Aspirations can be construed as pretentions, but that is the risk an ambitious school runs. To not aspire, as I see it, is a greater risk. The Academy seems hellbent on verifying that it is nothing if not an aspiring place.

Hard work, growth, excellence—these attributes create a driven institution, certainly one that however much distinguished is in harmony with other American institutions. They are hard to take issue with. Academy parents do not take issue, nor do their children, who can say about their anxiety for being admitted, "I was terrified that I was doomed to go to public school for the rest of my life." When new students and faculty have passed through the Academy's judgment gates, they exult in this victory. It is, however, an ephemeral exultation, for once past the gate, the work begins.

4

The Goodness of Teachers

AP: How did you happen to come here?

T-1: This is a famous school.

T-2: One of our teachers said a few years ago, "Teaching in Edgewood Academy is not a job, it's a way of life."

T-3: Well, they tell you when you come here that they want your life. I mean, I guess if I'm honest, they told me, basically, that they wanted my life. I guess I just didn't quite believe it. (She chuckles.)

T-4: I don't think there is anyone here who is not sincere about excellence.

AP: And what kind of coherence is there among this group as to what excellence means?

T-4: Very little.

T-5: You know, Ed [the headmaster] is the first person to say, "Take it easy, buddy, relax." But look at the guy. You don't see him kicking back in the halls. He's pretty driven. I think it comes out of a sincere effort to do a good job. Again, one of the things I have liked about this place is that I think there is not a lot of real cynicism about this being a joke.

T-6: I think there is a sense … I feel that I want people to know that I am doing a lot. I guess that is the normal thing … that I am working hard.

AP: Is that the same as doing your fair share?

T-6: Doing more than your fair share.

AP: Fair share is not even enough for you?

T-6: I don't worry about it because I know that I am always busy. I don't feel guilty about it, to tell you the truth. I guess I have grown a lot in that area.

I begin with teachers, this chapter's focus, the goodness they manifest, and its consequences, asking, "What do Academy students have when they have an Academy teacher?" From many months of interviewing teachers and watching them at work, I documented their intentions and deeds. The aforementioned epigraphs are a sampling; more will follow. They encompass the breadth neither of what teachers do nor think they mean to do. Just as Academy students are skewed toward the uppermost end of achievement, I skew my representation of the teachers, forgoing the picture that would result if I included here snippets from noneffervescent performers, those who, by some measures, are less than stellar. I focus on the stellar, for they, as I see it, are the norm.

The norm is elucidated and modeled by a headmaster who advises his teachers to take care of themselves, to not sacrifice their lives for the benefit of the Academy, but does otherwise himself. He arrives early, leaves late, and works tirelessly on behalf of the school he leads. The norm is underwritten by the efforts of teachers hired since the headmaster assumed leadership; they join those of their predecessors who work with comparable effort, intensity, and commitment. As a famous school, it can compete nationally for promising teachers. As a school "where everybody is wonderful," it can attract and keep these teachers and their student counterparts. As a noncynical place, where teachers reach for excellence and teaching is a way of life, parents can feel they do well by their children to encourage their enrollment. And yet, if the ethic of striving and excellence seeking and extrinsic motivation and more shades into the neuroticism of "no matter what you do, it's never enough," then what do you have? Another story to tell,[1] dealt with briefly in this chapter, but whose elaboration is not consistent with my intentions in this book.

Academy educators were born, raised, and educated in locations scattered throughout the country. Some attended independent schools; most did not. In

---

[1]The myriad costs of unrelenting striving in schools and elsewhere is a critical matter. In this book, I am more concerned about the educational injustice that is implied by the Academy's amplitude.

keeping with Academy requirements, all have a university background in their teaching subjects. Most were not trained as teachers to teach their subjects, but those who were usually began their teaching careers in public schools. Some left public school teaching in despair at constraints to their work that they attribute to bureaucracy, teacher unions, or insular, inept administrators; others left by the lure of opportunity, financial and otherwise, available at the Academy. With few exceptions, and those temporary, teachers have at least a bachelor's degree in their teaching subject; many departments have at least one faculty member with a PhD. Teachers earned their degrees at both comparatively little-known regional colleges and universities—Mount Union College, Winona State University, and West Texas State University, and at better known national icons—Harvard, Brown, Dartmouth, and Stanford. Whatever else they once aspired to be or were—monk, physician, lawyer, scientist, professor, musician—all share the challenges of pedagogy at Edgewood Academy that are created by the students of talent that the Academy attracts. Theirs is no ordinary assignment.

Department chairs do not instantly reject hiring those who have gone the conventional route to teaching through formal instruction in pedagogy. Still, for example, of the English department's 24 full-time faculty, only one, its chair recalls, "had formal education training as an undergraduate major." Another he identifies proudly as one who had "100% of his training in English literature through the PhD level," a second who "has everything but the dissertation in English Renaissance," and a third who did "undergraduate training in speech education and followed a master's program quite far in classical rhetoric." School board members of a rural school I studied some years ago told me what they looked for in the teachers they hired: lots of activities in college, no Cs in their teaching subject, and that was about it. Without realizing that they did, they almost invariably favored teachers with a rural upbringing. They knew whom they wanted to teach their kids and why. Those responsible for hiring at the Academy also know.

In the year following my fieldwork, Edgewood Academy hired 22 new teachers. The first issue of the school newspaper presented profiles of each of them. I offer a sketchy overview of a sampling of these newcomers in order to demonstrate whom the Academy can attract to its classrooms, and, of course, whom they found attractive, the outcome of each department's judgment process. Although I cannot attest to the quality of their teaching, I can show how they looked on paper. MB: a veteran educator hired to teach chorus and senior humanities, has toured as a soloist with the New Orleans Symphony. KH: a "dedicated musician," hired to teach English, is completing his PhD, and will also coach debate. DA: an Academy graduate, hired to teach geometry, has a degree in engineering from Duke. RF: hired to coach track and teach freshman weight training, has a PhD in exercise physiology. KV: a Stanford graduate hired to teach tenth grade English, writes short stories (one has been published), rides horses, and rock climbs. JR: hired to teach English, has degrees in documentary photography and American Studies, and has studied abroad in Kenya and Vietnam. The Academy admires versatility. Teachers who manifest a desire and talent for teaching are even more appealing if they are well-degreed, well-traveled abroad, and seriously pursue sports, hobbies, and avocations that substantiate their breadth of accomplishment, if not something that can be converted into an Academy-sponsored activity.

A prized Academy educator, herself a certified teacher, did not want to apologize for her former public school colleagues, but she thought that she could account for the superior performance of her Academy colleagues:

> I think they learn to be good teachers because they have the time. They have the time to prepare. They come to class prepared. They have a true desire to teach, rather than the necessity of finding any old job. They teach motivated students, which I think would bring out the best in a teacher. They also do not have to deal with the downside. They don't send kids to the office. They don't deal with petty discipline. They don't deal with kids cussing in class.

All this is familiar. It is the usual explanation for the success of elite schools. If it does not explain teacher passion for teaching or their willingness to persist in a job with seemingly unbounded expectations, it nonetheless captures some major distinctions among teaching ways of life. Missing from this teacher's picture is the significant matter of class size. Officially, the school notes its student-teacher ratio as 8 to 1. Actually, required subjects (e.g., English, mathematics, and history) may have 15 to 20 students. With a teaching load of four required classes and overall no more than a total of 60 students, Academy teachers are a world away from Horace and his compromises.

EXPRESSIONS OF TEACHER GOODNESS

I understand the work of teachers in one way based on what they say about themselves and their colleagues. I understand it in another way when I see what they do in their classrooms. When words and deeds are congruent, an observer can get a reliable sense of what the school experience is like for students in general. So if parents asked me what their child would have access to at the hands of Academy educators, I would say to read the section that follows. It presents at least a partial picture, partial in that I include only a handful of teachers, and partial in that there is more they should want to know about a teacher than I present in the following pastiche.

Academy students are able to study *art* with a teacher who says, "I'm somebody who's devoted their life to art, and I've been beating my brains out to stay active with it." *Mathematics* can be conveyed by a teacher who anticipates his forthcoming summer study of a newly acquired Geometer's Sketch Pad. The teacher enthuses about the potency of this new computer software, already imagining how students will be engaged by it. "So you can set up a situation and mimic a situation that I have never thought of before and I don't have the slightest idea what to say about that." "You like that," I say. "Oh, it is incredible." Among the *history* teachers is one (there are many more) who values classroom discussion when it goes into such "depth that you realize that all the usual surface explanations are such equivocal simplifications of extremely complex reality. That's certainly the agenda I have as a history teacher." A *physical education* teacher speaks of aiming students "toward lifetime activities, so that instead of a kid coming in and playing a game, they might ride the bike for half an hour, they may use the rowing machine, they may do the stair stepper, they may take a run. This is where we aim: to give them the idea of keeping fit for a lifetime." One Academy worthy tells me that "I come every day and I'm excited about what I'm doing. I come at 6:30, and I'm busy all day. I prepare for my classes and grade papers. The papers are, for the most part, interesting. I love what I do. I love closing the door and coming in here and doing my thing." Her "thing" is teaching *English. Foreign language* instruction is available from a teacher who says, "I don't have any desire to be a college teacher. No offense. I like to teach. I like to be in the classroom. I like to be challenged. I like to fail so that I can do better, cry about it a little bit, and then say, 'Shit, what am I doing wrong?' I mean, I like that. I don't like it when it's easy for me." Finally, in this splurge of self-representations, Academy students can study *science* with the teacher who talks about good days in class, savoring such days, but always thinking that what was good can be better, believing that such an outlook fits the nonstatic, evolutionary spirit of his school.

Students learn a plethora of intended and unintended things in school. I thought of this most particularly the day I walked into a classroom with a teacher, both of us 10 minutes late. The scene as we entered was of students engaged singly and in pairs preparing for the day's work. Everyone was engaged; there was no one to play with in the usual way when a teacher is not present. The teacher explained that this did not happen naturally; it took intent and effort. Accordingly, students learned about self-control, responsibility, engagement, initiative, and autonomy, in addition to whatever else they learned that was in the lesson plan for the day. And I thought of this again the day I received a teacher's e-mail message that was sent to all Academy faculty and staff. It related to the school's sixth grade, not a part of the Academy that I studied, but the message is too good to pass by:

> In 6th [grade] philosophy we sometimes chew on a single sentence for weeks. A particularly tasty morsel this year has been the quotation, "Freedom is the luxury of self-discipline." Bally thing is, we can't remember who said it, so 6th graders are attributing it to everyone...Anyone know the real source?

Whatever else they learned about freedom and self-discipline, students experienced intellectual persistence, the play of ideas, and involvement with abstraction and uncertainty.

Other teachers offer other morsels. Here is a succession of English teachers, one at the sophomore level, preparing to teach *Romeo and Juliet* but delaying the moment with his own joking, acting, and teasing, in which spirit the students soon join him, and as quickly vacate when the teacher signals that it is time for the ill-fated adolescent lovers to take over. Lightheartedness and seriousness are amiable companions in this classroom. The teacher does not lose good time returning the students to seriousness, and the students get a lesson in self-control, devotion to task, and playfulness. Juniors get another lesson from the teacher who welcomes them to class and hands out a page of instructions for the work of the entire period. The page contains a long quotation from Dylan Thomas and a request that they read it carefully several times and then write an essay that defines "the different attitudes or reactions of the speaker to his experiences on this particular day." Here is a segment of Thomas's first long sentence:

> It was a shooting green spring morning, nimble and crocus, with all the young women treading the metropolitan sward, swinging their milk-pail handbags, gentle, fickle, inviting, accessible, forgiving each robustly abandoned gesture of salutation before it was made or imagined …

This assignment brings to mind the swell of language—vocabulary, style, composition— students have daily access to during all their Academy years. I think, therefore, of what they have access to now and all the years of their life because this teacher did not hesitate to invite her students to wonder over how Dylans's "Delicate carousel plashed and babbled from the publichouses … "

Seniors come to class one day and learn that their teacher will be gone for a week, during which time they are to write an "interpretive paper" based on one of three plays: Henrik Ibsen's *A Doll's House*, Mark Medoff's *When You Comin' Back Red Ryder?*, or August Wilson's *Fences*. Her minimalist instructions impress me. The date of this assignment is mid-February, so the students have had ample time since school began in September to learn what this teacher expects in such an essay. Of course, the teacher builds on years of previous instruction by many other teachers who expected students to develop and manifest intellectual autonomy, deliberation over text, and the creation of their own text—their essays.

I offer another example of pedagogical "riches," this one from the school's crowning class, senior humanities, a compulsory course taught always by a pair of teachers drawn from a pool of English, history, art, and science teachers. In a weekly meeting, truly a seminar, the ten teachers of this course plan and evaluate their work; the syllabus changes accordingly. The class's mixture of literature and philosophy is far from every student's taste, but they have no choice except to soar or muddle through a year-long thicket of ideas, challenges, and language. By April, the syllabus brings students to Nietzsche's *Thus Spake Zarathustra*.

Here are segments from a section jointly taught by an English and a history teacher. The class is a pedagogical mixture of students reading from the text and paraphrasing what they read, teacher questions, and student speculations about what the teachers asked. Smack in the middle of reading a section, a student stops himself and interjects, "God, how I love Nietzsche!" A teacher says she is not sure what Nietzsche is saying at one point, but then asks, "Is the herd essential?" A student answers that "He really is the philosopher of the few, which I find more interesting and compelling. He's saying there is an amorphous herd, so stay out of its path and do your own thing." This said, he turns adolescent and eats one of the two Twinkies he brought to class. A teacher asks, "How do you despise as only lovers despise? Another of Nietzsche's paradoxes." A student wearing a blue baseball cap placed popularly backward on his head expands on the nature of lovers, as he sees them.

In another section of senior humanities, the teacher ends the class by telling students that he walked to school that morning in the cold "as Nietzsche would want me to." He mentions the parody he wrote in preparation for a forthcoming faculty meeting on restructuring. He reads from his parody: "The administration is dead and we have killed it. Who will wipe the blood off it?" I do not learn what the students make of this teacher's walk in the cold and his little parody, beyond the fact that their teacher, not unknown or dead persons, writes parodies, and that he, in jest, connects what he does to what Nietzsche imaginably would have *Ubermenschen* do.

Occasionally, all sections of senior humanities come together as one large group. When violinist James Buswell visits the Academy for 2 full days in residence, they assemble to hear Buswell discuss Wagner and Nietzsche. During his visit, Buswell offers master classes and meets with the school's many music groups, and also with the Russian class to discuss Russian composers and performers. Throughout the year, the Academy hosts visitors from the academic and performing arts worlds for a day or longer.

WHAT TEACHERS DO AND WHY

At best, our teachers love children, love teaching, love their school, and possess the talent, energy, commitment, experience, and learning to transform their love into exceptional daily classroom practice. This is not a prelude to documenting an established reality that approximates this ideal in the conduct of Academy teachers. It is, however, a preface to acknowledging that what I learned about these teachers does bring to mind the prospect of such an ideal, a prospect that is vivified by listening to teachers and their students, and watching them at work. (Having imagined this ideal, I think, why not? Why should parents, why should anyone, settle for lesser standards?)

Through interviews, I accumulate the self-reports of teachers. I learn, for example, that the annual statewide science fair involves students and teachers in weeks of preparation. Finding time to meet is complicated at the Academy because most students, as I discuss in the next chapter, are outrageously busy, as are the teachers. "When do you actually meet with the students who will participate in the fair?" I ask a science teacher. Her answer: before and after school, lunchtime, the beginning or end of class periods, in the hall, on the sidewalk between buildings. The activities of the science fair, she explains, lead students into "all kinds of hands-on activities. I find I really enjoy seeing these students do these things." By really enjoying, she uncomplainingly makes herself available during the many jots of time when the students are available.

Another teacher feels loved by her students, and loves them in return. When she was sick and out of school recently, students called to "make sure that I was ok." For my benefit, she elaborates what her teaching is like, what types of activities she thinks her students find interesting and important. The more she talks, the more she warms up to seeing herself exuberantly present in her classroom. It was as if she had never before quite seen herself as she now did when she burst out with, "I *love* teaching. I *thrive* on being around teenagers. I think they are active, they are intense, they are growing—*that* is why I teach."

At the Academy, who arrives early and who stays late is known but not necessarily commented on. It is too common. I ask about it, wanting to know how teachers explain such behavior. "It is necessary just to get your work done," I learn. "But other than that, sure, it's love for the place and you want to do your best," which factors, I think, are an essential complement to the getting-work-done explanation.

More telling than what teachers say about their work habits and feelings is what students say about their teachers. Here are the impressions of four students. They offer uncoerced praise of teachers, their comments a response to a long series of terms I gave them to react to. In the first several months of my association with Edgewood Academy, I heard many offhand remarks about the school and its teachers. I then used these remarks as stimuli for interviewing students and teachers. One of them was "teacher dedication." After mentioning these words, I'd ask, "To what extent does this describe teachers as you know them?" Students answered:

I think "conscientious" would probably be a better word. Most of them seem to care and seem to be concerned about what they're doing. They give you time when you want to see them. I'm generally impressed with that.

I think each teacher is real dedicated. ... Their classes usually go somewhere, they usually make sense, and they don't give us tasks to do just to waste time. ... I see most of my teachers out of class usually going somewhere, but it's not like goofing off, or something. It seems like they're either involved with some extra-curricular activity, like the Educational Policy Committee, or something, but, yeah, I have a sense that they're bigger than just the person they are in class.

If you get a good grade, they will, like, write you glorious comments, but teachers are more worried about the people that get bad grades. They honestly make an honest effort to help you. They will learn what your schedule is and say come to my office and talk about it. They will make the effort. They will go that extra four or five miles. They will sit you down and say, "Listen, you are having a major problem in my class. Here is what I think you should do."

For every student that stays up until 3:00 in the morning writing a paper, I also see the teacher staying up until 3:00 in the morning grading them. I think they'll put in as much as the student puts in, or more. I've never had busy work. It's always something different, something challenging.

When I learn about the teachers and their orientation to work, I am not surprised to hear such praise. From teachers I hear utterances of a perfectionism that may be an Academy commonplace: "There are times," a teacher muses,[2] "I have a class where I think I could have explained the work better. That motivates me to look again, looking at how I might be able to improve it. Just this week there were three times I revisited something because it wasn't clicking for the kids." A colleague joins her in even stronger perfectionist language: "I would hate to think I have taught the perfect class. I would hate to think I have had the perfect course. I would hope that I can always do better."

Perfectionism is the companion of overextension and workaholism; indeed, all three may be one and the same, the difference being only in the preferred choice of words teachers select to describe themselves. Teachers who have taught elsewhere know they are busier at the Academy than they have ever seen teachers be—"I have never been at a school where there's so much extra going on, and so many requirements of one's time outside of class. We really are, most

---

[2] I use *muse* intentionally here because this is what teachers and others do when I ask them to tell me about their lives as teacher or counselor or administrator, and after we have been talking over a period of months. Needing to know what they do and what it feels like to do what they do, I invite them to talk about themselves in a way that most often they have never talked before. Quite properly, they muse.

of us, overachievers." Workaholism is epitomized in this teacher's unapologetic self-portrait:

> I think you say no, or should be counseled to say no, in those situations when saying yes is going to be detrimental to you. At the moment, it is true, I am chairing the Senior Appraisal Committee, on the Educational Policy Committee, assisting the dean and occasionally the headmaster on special projects, teaching sixth grade, and coaching the eighth grade boy's basketball team. There may be a couple of other things, but those are the main things. But I enjoy all those; I don't resent any of them.

A teacher spoke of the workaholics as Academy "heroes," adding that "there's a reward for killing yourself." He learned from the professional counseling service available to all Academy employees that "everyone who comes here [to the service] from the Academy says that the level of expectation is *so high*."

The ubiquity of this intense work ethic was not just the talk of my interviews. It was so characteristic of Academy teachers that it inspired the head of the school's counseling program to send this memo to her colleagues. She began with a quotation from an e-mail message she had just received, and then made a suggestion and a revelation about herself:

> "I still think the model employee is the person who will sacrifice home, family, and life for EA. If that is even remotely true then it seems that you have to get sick to survive … This is really a matter for a faculty forum … " I would love to devote a faculty forum to this issue. I would even be glad to moderate it … I continue to struggle to find the healthy balance in my own life between Academy-related and non-Academy-related activities. Both are absolutely essential. I wonder how much is my own intense personality and how much is the press of the institution that moves me toward an unhealthy balance.

A moment after she sent this e-mail she received one back that began, "Great idea, except that no one will have the time to attend!"

Institutions have rules and regulations, a mission, norms, as well as a culture that shapes, inculcates, rewards, and punishes the behavior of its participants. Says one of the Academy's most veteran teachers, "The thing about this place is that it never stops. It is a very high intensity kind of place." Some faculty, he thinks, can get away with just teaching their classes, but "that is not typically the norm."

What the norms are at any particular time may enjoy a consensus, but it will not do to expect precision about what exactly they entail. Norms result from the interaction of what institutional authority formally proclaims and what those to whom the proclamations apply make of them. At the Academy, it is illuminating to begin with its headmaster. Though he is not often physically visible to his faculty, his charge to his faculty and his modeling are most palpable. Excellence, as previously noted, is his standard; its application has no limits. For example, when the matter of high standards arises in my discussion with a department chair, he elaborates that they are:

> very, very important. If we are what we purport to be, than we should have and continue to have high standards. [*AP*: "Where do they come from?"] Top down. It would be a hell of a lot easier for me not to work as hard as I do in my classes, but if I didn't [work hard], I'd be hearing about it fairly soon. You know, I'm starting to learn that that is part of my role in the department. If I see somebody whose standards I am not impressed with, I would be compelled to sit and talk with them about it.

The headmaster models ceaseless, energetic activity. Perhaps there is no more fundamental manifestation of these facts than in the school's hiring. Of course, job candidates are not asked if they are driven, overachieving workaholics. Of course, those doing the selecting look for persons who will fit—themselves, the students, the school, all that makes up this striving institution. They find them, as the words of several newly hired teachers verify: "You know, I just push and push and want to get better...I believe in excellence." And from another: "I'm so good at compounding expectations for myself … " "Self-imposed?" I ask. "Yes. I mean, I'll look for work."

Given the nature of the teachers the Academy hires, perhaps a good deal more than half the battle of maintaining striving, driven behavior is won. The headmaster has strong allies in this cause, particularly from among his administrators, the deans and department chairs who are the direct agents of his plans and expectations. Again, hyperbole is easily come by when I learn about administrators. I would never think of being an administrator at the Academy, one teacher tells me, "unless I start liking 16 hour days and weekends, coming back after dinner, which is quite common, coming in at 6:15 in the morning, which is quite common, working weekends, which is quite common." Another teacher describes one of everyone's favorite administrators: "He lives here, absolutely lives here. He's here every weekend. He is praised for it here. He is promoted for it here. And he chose it, he chooses to live like that. That is what is really held up here."

These excelling administrators are responsible for the range of defining, implementing, clarifying, enforcing, disciplining activity that is carried out on behalf of the school, their department, and the students. In short, they are pivotal actors in the Academy's prevailing organizational press. They oversee their teachers' short- and long-term performances.

With the grail of excellence held aloft, teachers must aspire broadly, their conduct assiduously scrutinized, their salary increases and, they often believe, their jobs dependent on the judgments of formal evaluative scrutiny. In short, Academy teachers must be good beyond their classrooms, their goodness visible and thus verifiable. Beyond being seen as triumphant knights of the classroom, they must be ardent pursuers of scholarship, as manifest in attendance at and participation in professional meetings, workshops, seminars, and short courses. They must apply for, and sometimes win, the prizes of competitive scholarships and fellowships that take them to universities and programs around the country and overseas, as well.

A relatively new teacher presents her sense of what she perceives that the Academy wants her to do, a sense she acquires from what she learns and what she sees other teachers do. I call this the organizational press:

> Asking that question, "How can I improve upon what I do here?" that's the sense that I get. I don't see people stagnating here. I get this sense that they want people who are forward thinking. [*AP*: "Where does this sense come from?"] I think the most obvious ways have been through the evaluation process. I heard it in my [job] interview. It keeps coming up. It's not something that's said and then is put back in the drawer. I think it's one thing to say we want you to grow professionally, but to back it up by having money I think definitely communicates that, "Yep, we want you to do this and we're going to make it possible for you to do it."

Of course, Academy teachers coach, but coaching does not consume them as it did in the days before Mr. Compton took over. Today, their service obligation is broadly defined. In one department chair's view, service is everywhere:

> Service to the Academy can consist of visibility in the community beyond the school; visibility that is effective redounds to the Academy. Examples are membership on boards of philanthropic organizations, membership in service organizations, teaching a methods class at the university. Service to the Academy is the extent to which the person's presence and influence extends beyond the classroom. We look for significant service and support of the total educational program, coaching, sponsoring various student organizations, service on committees, special educational groups, advising, etc. So a teacher whom two dozen students elect as their advisor annually is providing strong service to the Academy. That's not scholarship or teaching, that's service to the Academy. A teacher who makes a distinguished contribution to the diversity committee and does nothing else might be regarded as rendering strong service. So that person doesn't coach anything, that person does not time athletic events, that person just goes and talks with colleagues about diversity issues. If I did distinguished service as a peer evaluator on evaluation teams, that would surely qualify as A-level service to the Academy.

This administrator's account of service dramatizes the reality of the formal service expectations that structure a teacher's professional life. Unsurprisingly, informal circumstances also affect the teachers, those things that they assume are true and act on accordingly, and also those things that regularly occur that are incorporated in behavior but not in the *Faculty Handbook*. I learned about the informal structures when I presented teachers with another term that I had been hearing in one form or another. (I wrote about *teacher dedication* earlier.) This term was "expected to say yes, learning to say no." "Alan," a teacher responded, "that's a neat term. I am caught up in this now. I was asked to chair a committee and I don't know how to say no, and I don't know if I am expected to say yes." The issue of saying no is the fear, one teacher said "the paranoia," that if you do, you will jeopardize your salary increase, if not your job, notwithstanding that "I have never seen an instance of it [job loss] happening." What teachers know does happen is that "if you never did say no, you would receive pats on the back." Put another way by another teacher, "The more you do, the more they want you to do." And by a third teacher, "If they see enthusiastic participation, they don't want to dampen it," meaning that if you are working zealously, extensively, and well, you will not be discouraged, even if by nonschool measures you should be. My respondents do not specify the identity of the "they" they refer to even when the speaker is a department chair and a likely "they." It is understood that they—the institution's gatekeepers of goodness—define it, look for it, and reinforce it.

Finally, a component of the organizational press is what I think of as the multiplier effect of teachers working in a certain way, getting rewarded for doing so, and, in time, creating a work climate that normalizes and perpetuates a particular way of working. This normalization is institutionalized in teacher, not just administrator, expectations of their fellows: "You don't have to volunteer for everything but you do have to find some way to reach out and show concern for other people's problems here if you are going to be a part of the community." Put more directly by another teacher, "There's sort of a group norm here of being a good guy, being a team player, being selfless, being a good sport."

Another aspect of this multiplier effect is the pace of teaching, so that the mathematics teachers who have been at the Academy for many years see how many of their students are "out of phase." This means, for example, eighth graders doing tenth grade work, or calculus students so advanced that now the school offers three different calculus classes, two of them at the advanced placement level. This happened, explained a teacher, because of the leadership of the department head, because of parental pressure, and because "I think there's an institutional commitment to doing as much as you can." The consequence of a faster pace of teaching, whether from internal or external conditions (advanced placement examinations), is pressure on the teacher to do more and do it faster, with no sacrifice of depth or quality. A teacher with experience in other schools says she has never taught anywhere else at such an "extremely fast pace. You feel like you never get caught up. And with bright students, you want to cover more material faster in the prescribed period of time."

There is about the Academy, a veteran teacher tells me, "a series of competing excellences." "Read the e-mail," she advises me. "I mean, the teacher in the speech department just won nationals. The athletic department just won state championship. The science teachers just won whatever they just won." Her fellow teachers, she thinks, get sucked into the consuming excitement of extreme achievement.

A GOODNESS COMPETITION

During a short visit in the spring semester before I came to Edgewood Academy for the full school year, I was standing on the sidewalk between classroom buildings confused about where to go that I would not be an intrusion. My research site was uncharted territory. This is often the case when I am getting started and do not yet know where I will be welcome. I was unsure where the lunchroom or the auditorium were; I did not know my way around in any sense. The sidewalk seemed safe enough. A friendly teacher came by, introduced himself, and stayed to talk for another 30 minutes. What I learned from him would, in time, prove invaluable. I explained what had brought me to his school and asked for advice about the teachers and students, what they were like, what he thought was important for an outsider to know. He stressed what I have already described, that his colleagues were exceptionally hard working, so that I needed to learn about the hours they devoted to school activity beyond their schedules and their assignments.

In light of what he told me, I asked if the Academy harbored what sounded like an ongoing "goodness" competition. He instantly affirmed that it did, and that it extended to both curricular and extracurricular matters in the form of empire building for getting the best students in your areas of work. He thought that speech and debate activities were a prime example. A few years back, they were minor activities, but now their budget rivals that of athletics, and after winning a national championship recently, they have lured students away from other activities such as journalism.

Teachers and administrators were quick to disclaim a goodness competition that embraced everyone, but they quite uniformly acknowledged its existence, including, beyond what I knew to ask about, winners who could be taken as candidates for sainthood. The competition embraced many facets of school life:

> Yes, there is a competition—I think it is a private school thing—in terms of working up the ladder, trying to get that dean's job, coaching so many sports, getting the most advisees, how popular you are, how hard your courses are, how

many papers you grade, when you get here in the morning, when was the last time you missed a day of school. There are people who brag about never having missed a day of school, even though they were desperately sick. What the hell is that! I don't think everybody buys into that.

And probably nobody very consciously buys into sainthood. Yet there are the Academy icons, the great teachers who are revered for their scholarship, their devotion to students, and even their eccentricity. "I'm sure there are many people who would love to find themselves in that role. I think there's a longing to be loved here. There are people—it seems like they're all dead—who are remembered with great love. I think there is a great desire by many to be loved on that level, to have touched everyone enough to be thought of that way."

Nobody I spoke with even vaguely indicated that they themselves were in a goodness competition, let alone sought sainthood. Yet, I heard often about those who already were candidates for canonization, and not all of them were dead. They were teachers who virtually lived at the Academy. Though they knew they could say no, they seldom did. Moreover, what they did, they did with alacrity and aplomb. If they did not consciously seek the respect of students and colleagues, they had earned it. Along the way, they set a standard that was stratospheric.

COSTS OF GOODNESS

Edgewood Academy is a heady, high-powered, exciting school, replete with challenges to one's talents as a teacher, counselor, coach, and administrator. The concomitant of these attributes at the Academy, as it is in other elite institutions, is pressure—to perform, to excel, and to grow. The merely good does not deserve mention; the better is for those getting started or who don't know any better; the best is the only standard worthy of the Academy. And the currency of best, its necessary condition, involves commendable educating in the broadest sense. Yet if strangers to the Academy knew only what I write about in this following section, they would rightly wonder why anyone would stay, high salaries notwithstanding.

I begin a consideration of costs with some personal accounts, none of them by teachers who gave any indication that they were ready to change jobs. Not meaning to leave, however, is not tantamount to being fully happy with one's conditions of employment. Moreover, although all teachers experience costs of one type or another, they perceive them differently, the youngish, new teacher with small children, for example, seeing them one way, the much older, veteran male teacher with grown-up children seeing them another way. They have the same job, undergo the same organizational press, but they are at different times in their personal and professional life.

John, a senior teacher, well-established in reputation, visible and appreciated in school affairs, speaks of the peculiar way being an Academy teacher can seize one's life:

> I really did have to go through a routine myself of how I felt as a person, as opposed to how I felt as a person teaching here. If you are a teacher teaching at this place there is a danger that you can ... if you say you are a teacher at Edgewood Academy, all of a sudden people are, "Oh! That's more like being a professor, really better than being a professor at the local university." That can have a real insidious effect. It gets harder, speaking personally, it can get harder to separate your role as a teacher from your role as a human being. The natural course of events is that you become much more of a teacher because you are not much of a person outside of here. So, it ends up just swallowing you all up.

John identifies the seductive hazards of one's prestigious position as Academy teacher, and the consequences of being swallowed up. It is this outcome that contributes to creating the school as a total institution (Goffman, 1961), and it is this structure that ultimately engenders the Academy's all-encompassing impact. In Goffman's usage, the term typically applies to the often malevolent, usually involuntary institutions of prisons, monasteries, mental institutions, and concentration camps, less typically to boarding schools and fundamentalist Christian schools. Twenty-four hour daily control of both physical and mental aspects of the participant's lives is the central attribute of the total institution. Walls, rules, and guards exist to insure the control, but where they do not exist, their effects can be attained by other means, as can be inferred from what teachers say about their lives as Academy teachers. High-level institutional commitment and loyalty help to establish and perpetuate the circumstance of a total institution.

Rachel is a fortyish, still junior teacher, with enough years at the Academy to have proven herself as accomplished both in and out of the classroom. I see no hint of her involvement in any type of competition, but she believes that she once worked like the swallowed-up Academy prototype of goodness.

> I know that I became at one point totally involved with the school in the sense that I was practically living here. I might just as well have moved in. Nobody ever saw me at home. Nobody ever saw me anywhere else. I was always here. A lot of that was due more to my extracurricular activity combined with the course load I had. I just didn't have enough time to get everything done. That does become addictively detrimental to your family. I would say I probably did it for 2, maybe even 3 years. And then decided ... I just sighed and I said, "Wait a minute. This is not working. I have to reorganize."

Working in a way that earns plaudits reinforces working that way. One gets addicted to an additive pattern of doing well, doing more, and doing everything one needs to do for the job.

Tracy, with one young, preschool son and a marriage under 10 years old, has taught at the Academy almost as long as she has been married. She likes her school and hopes her son will be able to attend. In fact, for the students, she applauds the school's academic virtues; for herself, the picture is less praiseworthy.

> Working here … it kind of goes back to that whole business about getting overextended, getting too many irons in the fire, and getting too many conflicting agendas and not enough time to deal with anything effectively. Then you go home and you're in conflict because you haven't done enough with your family. It's a constant for me. We [she and other teachers] talk about it all the time, about trying to balance and to say no and to make it smooth. There's always been this feeling that your family doesn't really exist here, your outside family. You don't talk about your outside family, you don't talk about your spouse, you don't talk about your children.

She works with verve, students clustered around her, looking like she is happy to be just where she is—engaged with students. Her husband does not understand that the Academy job is a self-perpetuating vortex of involvement. His wife does what comes naturally for her as an Academy teacher.

Cora is a divorced mother of one middle-school child, a senior Academy teacher, one of the stalwarts whose substantial contribution to the school makes it difficult to imagine an Academy without her. It is the end of May when she makes these comments:

> I have not gone out on a date since February or March. By the time Friday night comes along I am usually too tired to go out. The last four weekends in a row for me have been involved in something at the Academy. Yeah, I really have no life outside the Academy. You may have to be a little crazy to work here. In fact, I was talking to a teacher here yesterday. We talked way out in the parking lot because we wanted to make sure nobody heard. He said, "Why do we subject ourselves to this place?" I said, "I am going to be 37 in a couple of months. Maybe it is a midlife crisis, but especially as a single parent I just can't say I'm burned out, I am going elsewhere. I need the salary. I have a kid to support. So I will put up with far more. It is survival for me." I have heard of male faculty sleeping in their offices and showering at the gym. So marriages are in serious trouble. You come up here any time, day or night, and there are cars in the parking lot and lights on in offices. I don't know what these people are doing here at 2:00 a.m.

Perhaps faculty members with spouses and children can remain at work all night. Cora cannot. But she can manage to work extensively over four consecutive weekends. Academy teachers are able to visualize work that they think must be done, almost without limits as to when it will be done. This way of working is not mandated by their contracts.

At the Academy, if teacher goodness is one side of a coin, teacher stress is the other side. When I attended an all-day teacher workshop on diversity the spring before my year at the Academy, I heard a teacher, a veteran of 7 years, praise the school in grander terms than I'd ever heard directed to any school. She concluded by speaking of her and her colleagues' stress, which she thought of as self-imposed. Thereafter, I would continue to hear about stress. A member of the counseling faculty thought that no less than 99% of the faculty were stressed as an ordinary condition. Toward the end of the school year, all faculty received this e-mail: "plans for tonight: pizza for those who want it; Sarah leading a discussion on stress; we'll be in the West Campus Dining Hall, 7:00 p.m.; Come if you feel like you need a big hug!!" Stress was too frequently mentioned for me not to incorporate it into my list of words to which I invited reaction: "Is stress part of the job? I asked. "Extremely. When I am around some of the other people, I think, 'ah ha, I'm not the only one.' I can see it in people's faces."

The culture of success, as some faculty see it, would persist at one level because of the teachers' pride, their great ability, and their commitment to their work. It reaches another level because of the headmaster's ambition for the school and its students. Some teachers point to the parents: "I'm paying $6,000 for my boy or my girl to go to this school. I want to see some results." Some spoke of the strain of working without tenure, waiting each spring for the letter that confirms if they have a job for next year and what their salary increase is. Some spoke of the unbounded nature of their job, a job without a job description, "so that people are always looking over their shoulders, constantly, like, is anybody seeing what I am doing, am I doing this correct, am I doing a good enough job to stay on here." A teacher says he knows "people here who do way, way more than they need to. I mean, far more, far more than anybody would ask them to. They [school authorities] don't make them not do it, but ... boundaries, that's always the difficulty, that you've got to establish them yourself, because nobody is going to do that for you. You can work 24 hours a day. I don't see anybody stopping that."

Stress was so commonplace that until it got extreme toward the end of the academic year, teachers spoke of it matter-of-factly. Stress had become normalized at the Academy, as commonplace as seniors being accepted by prestigious universities and colleges, and the boy's basketball team winning the state championship, as commonplace, perhaps, as disorder in a dysfunctional family.

"You have to create spaces of calm, aggressively," as one teacher described her sense of how not to "let the institution just sweep you away." And another said, "You note the irreverence in my voice. I love this place, but I have to be irreverent about it. It's the only way you can maintain some kind of balance. You can go off the deep end in this place." As a sort of total institution, the Academy elicits such strong responses. They are natural reactions to an institution that creates a crafty web, an overarching structure of filaments that ensnare the persons who came voluntarily to the web and by their own behavior prolong it. The web is comprised of high standards; high rewards for success; vivid models of success manifest by leaders and by the rank and file; explicit, systematic oversight of conduct in the exhaustive evaluation system; and so many occasions for performance that it is fairly said that no one can ever complete his or her work. Thus, there is bait in abundance to enter the web, and myriad forms of stickiness to insure that once entered, getting out requires major acts of will—that is, if one even wants to get out. For the web can become the primary place in one's life, so that as one is "consumed," one joins the "spiders" in their life of institutional goodness.

Total institutions are generally perceived as nasty places that contain the criminal, the sick, the overzealous—unwanted people, extreme people. To the contrary, Edgewood Academy, a service institution, does the educational bidding of a select population of academically talented youngsters and aspiring parents. Notwithstanding its admittedly exalted purposes, it functions somewhat like a total institution in the lives of its educators, who have entered by their own volition. Once having come, however, they are subject to a host of ensnaring structures that effectively claim their life unless they consciously, with determination and persistence, will otherwise. And, it must be added, once having come, they tend to stay, captured by the promise and fulfillment of being an Academy teacher.

5

The Goodness of Students

Honestly, I think there was much less work as an undergraduate in college than there was in high school here. I remember in high school just feeling sort of overwhelmed a lot of the time.

—Former Academy student

As members of an intensely academic community …

—Academy student newspaper editorial

> *AP:* What do you think the Academy takes very seriously in the education it offers you?
>
> *S:* Hmm, that 99% of their graduates go to college.
>
> *—Academy student*

There is nobody here that I know that couldn't succeed if they wanted to. There are very few people I know who couldn't excel if they wanted to. There are an awful lot of people who don't seem to want to excel. I guess that is ok, too. That is something that is almost impossible to weed out.

—Academy student

Four more days until I am out of this hellhole …

—Academy student

H igh schools are places of counterpoint, indeed, of proliferating, shifting, situational counterpoint, so that in the course of a day, week, semester, and year, students will cross and recross boundaries into contrasting, if not antithetical, domains of activity, expectation, and mood. Their traversing of domains—some of it institutionalized and thus required, some of it not and thus a personal choice—students eventually take as normal. They do not have to like what they do, and they can do what they have to do with varying degrees of enthusiasm, interest, and willingness. But however variable their behavior, they will be in classes that range across many cognitive domains, they will participate in extracurricular activities that also include the cognitive but extend as well to the athletic, artistic, and service activity, and in one way or another they will engage in the many social or interpersonal occasions that always are available to bring joy, pain, or both to adolescents.

The pristine elegance of the Academy's architecture and physical environment could lead to thinking that what money has constructed will have its counterpart in the behavior of its adolescent participants. Of course, this is foolish. Students are not pristine. Academy students are like other students, notwithstanding the selection hurdles they have leaped in order to gain admission. The school that is built around this academically skewed bunch of young people is, in many ways, recognizably an American school, yet its resemblance to other schools does not make it like other schools whose defining features are modest academic achievement, athletic obsession, and predominating social affairs. What follows, therefore, is what exists at Edgewood Academy, but is not consequential for my purposes.

> *Students steal.* A teacher's e-mail message contains the story: "I know we would all like to think that we are without thieves at E.A., but the facts stand for themselves." The "facts" were the three "major" pieces of audiovisual equipment missing from the library.

> *Students are unruly.* Another e-mail message from an administrator gently informed teachers that "as you may have noticed, the natives are restless today. Your presence in the hallways is much appreciated."

> *Students disrupt.* "Due to the recent misuse of water weapons in South Hall, we have a new policy regarding the use and/or possession of water pistols, rifles, balloons, or pressurized weaponry in South Hall. Beginning on Thursday, please confiscate any and all water propelling devices … "

Students abuse drugs. The Academy Newsletter informed parents of a Parent Awareness Night event that would be moderated by the school's Drug and Alcohol Awareness Team. The *Newsletter* raised several attention-getting questions: "Some Academy students are asking: 'Why are some parents so blind to what their kids are doing with drugs and alcohol?' ... Some Academy parents are asking: 'Am I over-reacting to what my teen and his friends do on weekends?'"

And *students get their hearts entangled*, as the writing of several younger students makes clear:

> I got asked to homecoming by a senior and am really excited about going with him, he's a really fun guy. I just feel really bad because my best friend kind of liked him and another friend asked him to homecoming; he turned her down and then asked me. I know it's not my fault and no one's mad, but I feel badly.

> Social life, ha!, that's a joke. Everything with my friends is going well, actually. But there are a few senior girls who are working pretty hard at trying to make my friends and I feel bad about ourselves. They write in the "Underground" newspaper about us. I better explain. A group of senior girls have been known as the slaves since they were freshmen, primarily because of their reputation with boys. They have never truly liked me or any of my friends because we got older boyfriends with some quickness last year. If they are upset because they are jealous, I do not know, but they are trying to put their reputation on us. Little do they know, we WILL get them back. Sounds petty, huh!? It is but that is the way sophomores are.

> The pressure for sex is ridiculous. You know, as a guy, sometimes, I really get pissed off cause it's, like, I'm a man, does that mean I don't get allowed any emotions. If you asked a sixth grader, "Are you a virgin, kid?" it would be, like, "no." It's ridiculous that people should feel shame. I was totally locked in shame about this time last year that I was still a virgin. Still am. Then I realized, you know, if I don't feel right about it ... I talked to some people. They're, like, you know, "it's really cool." But the pressure is there.

These are the matters of the one hand, the counterpoint that emerges from the nonacademic dimensions of life at every American school. They intrude, define, taint, energize and more; at times, their importance exceeds other matters. They never fully go away. The point of the other hand, the academic, is, relatively speaking, overwhelming. I am tempted to say that it is *the* business of the school, but I am not persuaded that I safely can because I believe that schools provide occasion for more than one business.

Academics, however, are unmistakably salient. Students enroll knowing that this is the case, and they receive reminders at every turn. The Academy produces information for the benefit of students, parents, and teachers that documents its academic pedigree. As a prep school, it does so naturally, a matter of course. Given the school's professed intention to be instrumental for entry to college and university, it provides information about its success in this regard.

So it is that I and everyone else learn that for admission to the ten top American institutions of higher education, as ranked by *U.S. News and World Report* in 1995, Academy students succeeded to this extent (The first number is the number of students who applied for admission; the second is the number granted admission.):

Brown University—9/5

Dartmouth—8/5

Duke—16/5

Harvard-Radcliffe—8/5

Johns Hopkins—2/1

MIT—6/3

Princeton—11/4

Stanford—25/11

Yale—6/2

No Academy student had applied to Caltech, the tenth institution on this list. In a fairly typical year, seniors submitted 553 college applications, receiving 419 acceptances, 104 denials, and 30 waitlistings; 104 students in all of New Mexico were named semifinalists in the National Merit Scholarship Program; 26 were Academy students.

PORTRAITS OF STUDENTS

These achievements seldom come easy. Hard work, dedication, and perseverance must accompany the ability students demonstrated they had as a condition for being admitted. To communicate what student life is like, I present portraits of five students, the first three based on my interviews with them, the fourth the product of a class assignment, the fifth also from an interview.

Doug—A senior

I get up at 6:00 and I have for the past couple of years. I have had conversations with other students on the phone at that time, usually school or extracurricular stuff. I have come to school at 7:00 in the morning numerous times to get things done. I have written many papers in the Mac labs at 7:00 in the morning. I have never come and found the buildings locked. The gym is open; people use the facilities to work out. Depending on the day, I stay here after school to get work done, but I frequently meet my girlfriend. We'll go back to her house and sit around and talk or sit around and read or do homework. These days after school there is science olympiad. We're gearing up for the state championship competition. If it's not the olympiad, it's something else to do after school. After supper, almost exclusively homework, usually from 6:30 to 10:30 or 11:00, but it's not nonstop work. On weekends, there are tournaments that will eat up all day Saturday, and that means I spend all day Sunday on homework. I guess I'm usually doing some sort of extracurricular activity on Saturday.

Doug has learned that there is almost no time during the day or week that is beyond devotion to school activity. His life is geared to a nonstop, school-related schedule that is required to complete class work at a standard that he has set for himself. Like most students, he has no weekday job. He does not need the money, but more than that, he is comfortable with a life that begins and ends with school.

Sally—A sophomore

There are snobs here, probably more snobs here than inner-city Detroit, but I don't know if snobs are rampant and breeding and controlling the school. Some of my friends are kind of superficial and I'm friends with them. In a small school you don't really have that much of a choice, and that kind of depresses me.

I want to have philosophical discussions with people that are my friends. It's kind of bothersome when I can't. But on the same token, people get depressed and disillusioned when they talk about philosophy all the time. Anyway, I think I mean I do. I really enjoy it, but at the same time, when I keep going on and on about it, I get into these mental trances of just being kind of, "Oh God, we have to analyze the whole world only to find that no truth exists, and blah, blah, blah." That just leaves me feeling really empty and just kind of pissed, and so I'd rather talk about Terry's new car and whatever.

My mind thinks that sitting back and becoming really involved with what kind of car I drive and how many figures my income is, is really terrible. At the same time, there's another part of me that thinks, "Hey, life wouldn't be so bad like that." I wouldn't mind not having to think about things, but then my mind says, "Omigod, that's disgusting." So, where does that leave me, you know?

That's the major reason why when I do get depressed that's why I get depressed, because I feel like I get on this tangent. I wonder if it's bullshit. At the same time, I would think if it was bullshit, I wouldn't even be thinking it, you know. There are certain people that are destined to have to think about things, and live the life of misery when they do think about things …

Sally is a model of the very young, intellectually oriented student who treats the issues her able teachers generate in class assignments and discussions as worth engaging beyond homework and exams. She digs into things, and in the course of her digging becomes confused by the immensity of questions that defy resolution. While she cannot help being aware of concerns at the level of money and Terry's car, she knows that that is not where she wants to pitch her attention.

Tom—A junior

They don't really teach morals here. Well, they don't say these are the right things. It's not like Sunday School, or anything. I mean, you learn about morals, and you learn about other people's morals. You learn about people and you learn about history and you learn about events. There's just a lot of learning going on. I guess for each student, they get something out of the curriculum. What I try to get out of it is I try to relate it back to myself, you know. I guess I want to be real open and kind of get the tools and the foundation to do whatever you want to do with it. I don't think they like racists. I don't think they want racists here, but you can have your own opinion. And, you know, they don't teach one opinion. They're pretty open and leave it up to you.

My progression from sixth grade to, like, where I am now, I think I did change a lot, but I can't really say how, though. I just know I moved somewhere. I just went somewhere for better or worse. All the information and all the ideas that I get from all my classes I really try to use outside of class. I think that's real important to not just leave it in the class and walk out and be someone else for your next class. Sometimes I just get carried away or I get so tired that I can't. I remember last year. It was kind of cool just to kind of like be in class and get all the stuff and then go out on the weekend and be around all these people and kind of hear like how they use the stuff in certain classes, and they didn't even know it, how they incorporated what they learned in class. Like last year, this discovery came to me how, whether we like it or not, whether we say we hate the Academy for its hypocrisy or whatever, in the underground [newspaper] you felt a lot of hatred for the Academy, but I don't think they would have come to that conclusion without what the Academy gave them, without the critical thinking.

So, I just look at these people on the weekend and I see like how much the Academy gave them, and what it gave me. Then I felt like a little wholer, like they weren't just two separate worlds, but that everything did connect.

It's not just the classes; I think it's being surrounded by pretty intelligent kids. This may sound kind of snot-nosed, but kids with a lot of money, who have a lack of, maybe, real problems, like getting food or having friends, they don't have to worry about the base needs. Maybe they have [time] to figure out more elaborate problems, more mental problems. Like they think about what's the deal about life or this or that. I guess they kind of get philosophical, you could say, because I guess they have the time and they have a lack of real problems. So, I guess you have intelligent people who are well off, who have time to think about philosophical questions. You're surrounded by all these kids with a great environment. It's pretty protective. I think the only thing that holds it back or inhibits it is just the idea of grades and making, like, colleges happy. That kind of gets in the way.

I have to keep thinking about the illusion of the long run to keep me going, but I have to keep in mind having fun, too. You keep this duality going all of your life of the long run and short. If you fixate on the long run, though, you lose the good things of today. Having fun means making connections to do good work in school now and how this helps me do good for society.

Tom loves to learn, and he loves to think about what he has learned as it relates to his life outside the Academy. Yet he is not a monolithic student, his interests confined solely to intellectual matters. In the best Academy tradition, Tom is an athlete and a participant in other school activities. In this breadth, he has much company, a fact that reinforces the ideal of broad-based development, of being and becoming this *and* this *and* this.

Clara—A sophomore

On this fourth day of the seventh week of my tenth year of school I am in a good mood. It is not to be said that I do not have a large quantity of homework, but I am trying not to worry about it. This past week I have had a minimum of two tests a day, and three of my teachers asked that I rewrite papers. I am desperately behind in my work and I feel a sense of dread every time I think of grades. I am, however, slowly digging my way out of the pile of things to do. Friday (tomorrow) will end "English" week, as I call it, during which I have been rewritting my English papers. Next week will be "Physics" week and hopefully I will be able to make up the five labs that are halfway done. Then, it shall be "History" week and Rousseau and Locke will invaid my mind. I have more time to work, though, because I am grounded for being late. But that is another story ...

Clara wrote this at the request of a teacher who wanted to get a measure of how students felt about themselves and their work at that time. What I learn about the nonstop work schedule of Doug, the senior, has its counterpart in the life of Clara, the sophomore, though she is much less experienced with the weight of work demands and their management. Clearly, however, she is burdened by all that she feels required to do. This fact permeates her life; it is one that she will most likely learn to live with.

Fred—A senior

I think a lot of people don't do the reading. I haven't done a good portion of it, really. I've done most of it, but not a lot of it. I'm supposed to have read a packet that the teacher gave us, and I haven't done it. You can't just sit there and not say anything when everyone … it's obvious what's going on. So, while the teacher was talking about entry points, where the philosophy really comes and what the author is trying to tell us really shines [out], I was just flipping through the pages and I saw a question that looked pretty good. I said, "There's something I was wondering about on page 179," and I started reading it, saying, "Now that really seems to me like it's an entry point."

And the teacher said, "Oh, yeah," and he went off for 10 minutes. I felt great. I generally read the stuff, but I know why people don't have to read it, because a lot of people here are intelligent enough that they can do that sort of thing. I mean, I've done that before. I've done things in class, where I haven't read the material, and I become the crown prince of BS, and teachers eat it up. I'm sitting there feeling like a million bucks because they think I have this amazing insight. That's something you learn how to do well here, which is unfortunate, I guess, from an academic point of view, but fortunate from a realistic point of view, because that's a lot of what goes on in the world, it seems to me.

It would be naive to think that any school does not have its Freds. There is student diversity in regard to sincerity of intent to learn and participate as a member of an intellectual community. High school as intellectual community? Yes, the Academy so aspires, but not narrowly and foolishly. Its educators understand their own and their students' limitations of interest and capacity for establishing such a community, while continuing often to perform as if it were possible to have one. In the meantime, schools become places for the development of teacher-outsmarting skills, and of understandings and insights that the school has no interest in promoting.

Students enter the Academy at the sixth grade already knowing that they have come to a mecca for acquiring the credentials necessary for successful college admission. As a counselor observed, "Maybe for half of the kids, going to a good college has been on the agenda since the beginning of time." Every long night of study for an examination, every weekend devoted to writing a paper, does not begin and end with the effort's connection to grades and college admission, let alone to a palpable awareness of the connection, as one student put it, between "getting into a good college and getting a good job, getting good pay, getting a good house—the American dream." Succeeding with one's immediate tasks, of test or paper to write, may be preeminent, but never too far behind the success measured by grades is the reason for getting good grades.

In out-of-class activities, the likelihood of intrinsic motivation—the genuine love of sport, debate, drama, or writing—may be higher than for in-class activities. But never far behind this motivation is what the students call "transcript packing." This involves students figuring out what will impress college admissions officers and getting involved in the right activities. A student recalled his conversation with another student about participation in a new organization:

> I asked him why he was joining. [I said] "I would love to have you [in the new organization] if you are a hard worker. It is not the best attitude if you are here just because it will look good on a college application." This thought process that I go through ... I probably wouldn't think this if I was any place else. "How much time will it take? Will it look good on college applications?" That is my thought process. I am a freshman, and I am not really thinking that hard about it. When I am, like, a junior, college application will probably be, like, the first thing. I don't know if I am going to be happy about it, but I know it is going to happen. I know it has to happen just because of the intense academic and future-minded atmosphere of the school itself and of the parents and students and your friends. When I was in seventh grade, we had a class meeting where the college advisor from the upper school came down and told us how to fill out a college application form effectively. When I was in seventh grade!

This young student can have a carefree adolescence, up to a point. He could not easily ignore what is essential about his life as an Academy student: a heightened, pervasive, increasing awareness of a certain form of success, as well as knowledge about the road to this success.

The "transcript packing" referred to is not a secret student activity, although students do not parade this fact about themselves. It is something that one does, and has much company in the doing at the Academy and in high schools throughout the country. Looking good for college becomes a criterion against which students can determine what to do: "Like in my schedule for next year, should I take another science because it will look good, or do I take another history course because I like it more?" And from another student: "You will get fifty kids to sign up to be on the school paper as seniors so they can say, 'Yes, I worked on the paper,' but they have no interest in journalism whatsoever, or speech and debate or theater."

This college-oriented impression management is embedded in the student's peer culture and thus is there, everywhere, to socialize younger students with college smarts, with becoming wise for the assault on admissions. Ever self-aware, students say that "there is a school culture that includes the norm that everybody works hard." And they tell me that "If I ever said, I don't care about college, I think I would be ridiculed by a large number of my friends." Former Academy graduates assure me that such a peer culture is not new:

I'd say the biggest motivation was college, getting in a good college. You had to live up to peer standards. Your standards became your peer standards. It was like this competitive marketplace. It wasn't like people were very outwardly competitive, but it was sort of like this unspoken thing. I know I felt it and I know a lot of other people around me felt it, like, that it was really expected of you if you're an Academy student.

The perpetuation of this peer culture derives from students buying into it because it works. This culture is built on the performances of students such as Larry, whom I asked, after he had detailed the extent of his ordinary activities, "Why do you do it?"

I put a lot of pressure on myself to do everything very, very well. I don't want to do a lot of things ok, or a couple of things well. I want to do everything well. In debate, I want to do fantastic, even though this is my first year. In diving, I want to win the state championship. I tied for it last year; I would like to win it free and clear this year. I guess I see a lot of things that I might be able to do, and I have to go after them. Maybe that's why I'm taking six classes. I guess I just feel this burning need to do really well. I came [to the Academy] being competitive. I think I am leaving more competitive. I think part of that is the school, and part of that is just sort of natural tendencies coming out in me.

Parents provide tangible motivation to succeed, sometimes to an extreme. Knowing how competitive college admission can be, they join, if not lead, their children to aspire to admission to a "good" college; parents exhort and agitate and pressure their children. A counselor distinguishes between families who "lay down the law" that only As are acceptable, and families who "have a fear that gets … it is a nervousness in the parents and the nervousness gets translated because it was very internalized so that the kids feel terrible if they are getting Bs [even though] the parents are telling you that the grades don't matter that much." Teachers are very much aware of parental zealousness, and they may take account of it in their handling of students who do not get an A.

If the kid is a complete goofoff, I will give him a D very happily. But a kid who is trying and is still pulling in the lower C or D area, I sit down with the kid and we write comments to the parent jointly. It is a problem every single time because I know there is going to be a parent who is going to really punish the kids. I feel like I have to protect my kids from their parents.

Another teacher's recollection of a recent exchange with his class illuminates why "handling" may be necessary:

Yesterday, I asked the students to have their parents see the work they had done. That's all I ask, 2–3 minutes, saying, "Look, mom, this is what I'm learning, this is what I'm doing." The kids said the only thing my parents want to know is what an 83 is. Is it an A or a B? Ok, I said, "Wait a minute. Tell them what you have learned: here are all the regular predicates. Look, mom, here are all the comparisons. Look, here are all the stem-changing verbs, here's the indicative mode, the imperative mode, the subjunctive mode. Here's my creativity and expression in writing." [*AP*: "How did that go over?"] They said, "Give me a break. You don't know my mom and dad. They want to know why I didn't get higher than an 85. And they say if you got an 85, why couldn't you get a 90?"

Students are frank about parental zeal, not pleased to have to deal with it, but explicit about its existence. They recognize that parental concern is not always misplaced—"For myself, I think that there are times when I slack off and I think, 'Oh, my parents are paying $6,000 to $7,000 for me to get to school, and here I am rambling on about idealism.' I ask myself, 'Where is it really getting me?'" Students recognize that parental reactions can be contradictory: "Well, like, my parents always say they'll never get mad at me if I get a bad grade if I'm trying as hard as I can, but, then, sometimes if I do badly on something, my dad will get all upset. … It just makes me feel so bad, like I disappointed them, or something." Students recognize that parental reactions can be subtle, as a recent Academy graduate recalls: "I never had anybody say I expect you to get good grades, but, at the same time, something like that was understood." And they know that parental reactions can be direct—"My parents are pressuring me into deciding what I want to do with my life before I go to college so I can work toward that major, work toward that graduate school."

THE COLLEGE FACTOR

Look at the office suite I occupy. Only the headmaster and the dean have more elaborate quarters. I don't think that it is an accident, and it is not because I am here. Obviously, it is because the college advisor is here. You walk in here with your kid and this says to you that this is big-time stuff. One full-time staff person and a very elaborate physical set up clearly conveys by its size, shape, and location that this [college admission] is an important function of the institution.

—College advisor

College preparatory—that's in the title. It tells the parents, "Hey, if you want your kid to get in a good college, you can put your money on us." The school asks for a lot of money, so they have to give something back. They're not going to say, "Hey, you give us a lot of money, so we're going make your kid really understand how history relates to science." They don't promise that.

—Senior student

Clearly, the overriding reality of the Academy is the college factor. It is sustained by the almost unfailing, college-oriented desires and expectations of parents and students. Many students learn early about college. Here is the experience of Becky, a junior:

> Well, ever since I was about 8, people have been asking me where I wanted to go to college. The part of the Academy, the sort of upper middle class, like the families that have been here forever ... I was talking about it with a family friend. He was saying, "Well, where do you think you'd like to go to school? What region of the country?" I don't know if I want to go East, but I was thinking of maybe Boston. And he was, like, you can stay with Tommy, his son. When you go and visit, and things like that, you sort of set up things like that. I take all this for granted. I feel like it would be ludicrous if I didn't do these things. I mean, it would, like, be so against nature if I didn't go on these college trips. I have a lot of friends who have gone through the application process, and I know a lot about a lot of schools. I almost feel like it's an inherent part of my knowledge, sort of like instinct. I'm sure I just picked it up from when I was a little kid.

All that Becky has learned and known about for so many years does not relieve her of every tension and doubt associated with college admission, but it does significantly facilitate the process. The process is familiar to her; it holds no surprises. She can move confidently from tests to applications to visits to decisions, as she has seen friends and family members do. She and her parents are probably immune from the type of madness that has parents of sixth grade children asking teachers and counselors what classes their child should take that will give them the best chance for successful college admission. And she is probably immune from overreacting to the generally accepted fact that one's junior year transcript is the most important one. As one teacher said, "I teach junior English. You know, it's horrifying. They will rewrite a paper more often in junior English than any other year."

Becky introduced me to one large segment of opinion about the SAT test that every Academy student takes. The Academy publicizes how well its students perform on this element of the college-application process. Doing well reassures prospective students and parents, should they need more reassurance, that the admitted student will be in good company, attending a school where high test scores are the norm. Becky explains why the Academy offers no cram courses in preparation for the SAT examination:

> Cram courses—I think I would be offended if the Academy did that. Oh yeah, because I don't think that's what the point of it is. The point of it is to test your overall knowledge. I know that it's been questioned whether it's an accurate test, and I believe that it's questionable whether it's an accurate test. A certain group will do best on it because it's a prejudiced test. But I don't know, I just think it would kind

of be against the Academy's philosophy to have cram courses. It would be hypocritical, because if you're supposed to be, overall, teaching the brightest and the best, then why would they have to cram for a standardized test?

I asked many other students about the SAT examination. I learned that most do not take the privately offered, commercial cram courses, though they may purchase material that provides sample questions and answers. They also may decide to concentrate on vocabulary development, believing that a good vocabulary leads to better test results. Students never were casual about the exam, it was too important for that—"People were a little edgy the week before SAT time, but it was not like final exam week here." And they did not always do as well as they hoped to, so they did retake the test. But they seemed generally to feel that what the Academy taught placed them at an academic level above the SAT examination.

A teacher explained this as the students' snobbery about standardized tests in general. The consensus, she says, is that Academy students learn to think; standardized tests measure something less sophisticated and challenging that is ok for public school students, but not for them. "Teachers object to timed essays and multiple-choice questions, so much so that they didn't let students practice these skills in class. There is an attitude that public high school students take *AP* tests to assist them in getting into college, while Academy kids take them because their teachers insist they do."

From the time in the middle of their junior year until the time in their senior year when students receive the results of their several college applications, they are preoccupied with educational life after high school. They are not so distracted by this eventuality that they lose contact with their present life of classes, sports, and other activity. Still, for a protracted period of time, they are future oriented in a way that they have never before had to be. In company with thousands of students throughout the country, they are attuned to present acts and their relatively long-term consequences. If there is a difference for them, compared to students elsewhere, it is that Edgewood Academy organizes considerable activity designed to inform students and their families about the college admissions process. More impressive than the one-on-one meetings, the college fair, and the visits of numerous college representatives is an Academy activity that is identifiable as "bartering."

This term derives from Persell and Cookson's (1990) study of sixteen elite boarding schools (e.g., Phillips Exeter, St. Paul's, Groton, Kent School, Choate). They write that:

> Close networks of personal relationships between officials at certain private schools and some elite colleges transform what is for many students a relatively

standardized, bureaucratic procedure into a process of negotiation. As a result, they [the private schools] are able to communicate more vital information about their respective needs, giving selected secondary school students an inside track to gaining acceptance to desired colleges. We call this process "bartering." (p. 29)

Successful bartering depends on a high school's deserved reputation for regularly admitting academically talented students and on its resources and wit for hiring a talented, energetic college advisor who can establish a personal relationship with many college officials.

Edgewood Academy begins its process of advantageous bartering by its careful selection of students. It comfortably invests in the means to provide them the best available advice and information. Then it seeks an edge, nothing conceivably illegal, just ways that can communicate to colleges the most convincing picture of its students so that, other things being equal, Academy students will stand out. The Academy edge that most impressed me is the work of its Senior Appraisal Committee.

Four carefully selected members of the high school faculty join the college advisor in creating a portrait of each senior that will be sent to each institution to which students apply (and that each student receives personally from the headmaster). This is in addition to letters from individual teachers, coaches, and counselors. The portrait is the work of the Senior Appraisal Committee. It meets as a group for about 1½ hours each week beginning in September and concluding just before the Christmas break. Each member prepares a rough draft about two double-spaced pages long for perhaps as many as ten different senior students; the college advisor will prepare drafts for as many students as the rest of the committee combined. For all students there is a collection of information that is provided by their junior-year teachers, their coaches and club or activity advisors, but also by the students themselves. The rough draft crafted from this pool of information is submitted to the full committee for critique and redrafting. I attended these sessions. Like everything else the Academy does, the discussions I heard were intense, the participants skilled, and the school's high standards evident.

Among their many accomplishments, Academy students and teachers are verbally adept. They speak and write fluently, their ease and pleasure with language readily apparent. Perhaps no place more than at the meeting of the Senior Appraisal Committee is this adeptness displayed. "A few set the standards; the rest strive to measure up," is the opening line the committee agreed on for one student. "Delighted to be alive and participating in the world" is the quotation from a teacher that opens the appraisal for another. The committee takes care to balance its characterizations so that the student who "is bright, disciplined and productive" is further and immediately also represented as "funny, warm and ingenuous." No college admissions officer is going to long entertain the thought that this student is a nerdy drudge, cheerlessly frequenting a library carrel, his skin a too-pale white, best friends only with the computer librarian.

The committee protects its credibility, appreciating that if the college recipients of their student portraits distrust their work, they end up serving neither the students nor the Academy. So they are cautious, meaning to be accurate and, at the same time, always nondamaging. I see this caution manifest in the concluding lines of an otherwise fairly effusive portrayal: "Once focused, Regina is a very creative and talented person." Which is to say, I assume, that Regina is not always focused, but when she is, and the portrait says not a word about the infrequency of her focus, she is a winner. Nondamaging truth telling is a major challenge, but one the committee is extremely well-practiced to meet. This skill is embedded in the continuity of the college advisor, who unrelentingly faces each new student portrait afresh, eager to pounce on the nuggets the teachers, coaches, and advisors serve up for each of the senior students, but always careful to do optimum justice to the student within the boundaries of veracity.

I read and listened with amazement at the appraisal constructed for an "average" student. To be sure, the Academy average is distant from the average of most schools in New Mexico or anywhere else. Still, the lad was average within his actual school context, and the committee plunged into word play that steered a course between accuracy and nondamage: "So our congratulations go out to Fred. We have watched him grow and we are proud of the product—thoughtful, sensitive, gracious, energetic, upbeat. We recommend him, confident that he will succeed in a collegiate atmosphere because we have watched him do so here." If Fred is not Ivy League material, he is a good bet for many other places. The committee is saying that, after all, if Fred could make it through the Academy's demanding collegiate environment, surely he can do the same at your institution.

In the course of months of planning, thinking, visiting, worrying, and calculating, Academy students become adept at managing the complexities of the college-admission process. Within the interstices of the school's formal curriculum, where the college admissions process is lodged, students may acquire skills to deal with and knowledge about themselves, other people, and institutions with potentially life-long benefits.

What they may not acquire is the product of a factor much discussed by teachers as missing. It is intrinsic motivation, a love of topic, class, or subject, possibly all three. Students so motivated charm their teachers, bring them cheer on otherwise dreary days when everything seems so ordinary, and encourage otherwise overextended teachers to continue being overextended. A veteran teacher speaks warmly of students who discover they love what they are learning:

The most exciting students come in with some evident ability to do something. They get involved in something and all of a sudden take off like a rocket. It doesn't matter to us what department. I think the biggest thrill, at least as far as I am concerned, is for a kid to discover that she has the capacity for real excellence and kick the living crap out of something, just get so excited that that is all she wants to do, just find it so inherently exciting to do it and to do it thoroughly and do it well.

That there are too few such students at the Academy bitterly disappoints some teachers. Given their own love for their subject, they long for students who will join them in reading, talking, and writing that manifests a comparable love. They do not think that such longing is an inappropriate expectation for Academy students, and they wish they knew better how to recruit students to intellectual adventure.

COSTS OF GOODNESS

I think the Academy wants to be able to say ... like there is this sheet and it shows what the last class had as their average for ACT and SAT. They want us to be above that.

—*Academy junior*

Sometimes I'll come home and say it's a miracle. I don't have any homework. All of my long-term things are finished and nothing to practice. I'm just going to sit here and watch TV, go to bed at 8:00, and do nothing. It's happened once this year.

—*Academy junior*

> *AP:* If I were a new teacher here, what would you advise me to expect from the students?
>
> *T:* You should expect that there will be a tension between your expectation and their fulfillment of it. They will expect you to expect a lot and my sense is that there is a pervasive resentment in the students, a feeling of stress and pressure about that expectation that will get acted out in lots of different ways. They want to make sure that they are learning what they need to learn, that it is a good class, and that they are going to come out equipped to do what they need to do, whatever that particular course is. They just wish there were a way that they could do it without feeling so bad all the time.

While their teacher wrote on the blackboard, students huddled together doing group work. They talked quietly, beyond the teacher's hearing. One student turned to Rachel and asked why she was grounded. Before Rachel could answer, a third student said, "Because she brought home a 99, not a 100." Not letting the joke stand, Rachel instantly clarified, "Because I didn't call home on the weekend." A place is known by the jokes it tells; they often reveal what is important, though not what is necessarily good.

One day, a teacher looked around the room at her students before she began her planned work for the period. Believing that she saw more unhappy faces than she thought she should, she invited the students to write a paragraph or two about how they were feeling. A girl wrote, "My life sucks! I'm flunking Spanish, well not literally, but to my father it is. My Chem teacher couldn't teach someone to blink, and I have 1½ weeks to change the world. Everyone wants 100% of me everyday!"

A teacher spoke of a parent she had just met during the annual meeting of parents of juniors to discuss college possibilities. The parent was so intense that she advised him to calm down and to let his daughter make some of her own decisions: "You know," the teacher told the father, "If you talk to her at all like you're talking to me, you aren't giving her a breath to make decisions. I mean, it's, like, drumming, drumming, drumming." Parental motivation transmutes into parental pressure, another norm in student life—"It's what is expected."

A school counselor says that it is "very common" for students to come see her as a result of the pressure to keep up, excel, and please their parents. For her students, the counselor says, there is an "eroding sense of never being able to be on top of things." Although managing usually to avoid the terrors of a place with cut-throat competition, the Academy has become a place where even its best students can say, "I always feel behind." This observation contains an external condition—the magnitude of the to do's that encompass a student's life, and an internal condition—how a student relates to this magnitude. During the course of a long talk, Tracy, a junior, makes the point:

We had a community service forum today. I feel like I should be doing all this community service. It makes me feel guilty. All these other people are doing stuff. They are getting [making] time out of their day to do it and I'm not. They do it after school, but I don't see how I could do that. I think I should. If they can find time, then I can find time, but I am always in [one or another sport] season from the time before school starts until it ends. I am obligated, like everyone else is. In sports I feel like I should be doing more. This is really crazy, but, like, for track, my coach wants me to weight lift all season. While you are doing the sport that you are doing, you should have a stream of activity of lifting. So that's, like, another thing. I always feel like I should be getting stronger. With school, I always feel like I should be doing more because I can never do all my homework. You can't do one assignment because you have something more important that you have to do. For history we have this huge book. I feel like after each chapter I should really go back … I want to, like, go back and make a list of all the important things and define them and do all the stuff. I never have time to do that. I just always feel that I should do that to get a better understanding. I want to remember it, not just for the test. I want to, like, keep it with me. It's frustrating. I feel like I am learning so much and it just goes right out the other end.

Tracy gets excellent grades, competes in different sports all year long, and participates in other extracurricular activities. She is an Academy icon, albeit a frustrated icon. She epitomizes the Academy norm of always feeling besieged by too much to do. After listening to her recital of energetic abundance, I asked if she ever found time to read a book not required for any class assignment, a question that reflects my personal need to always be reading something that has nothing to do with the "assignments" of my life. Tracy responded with the obvious, "I don't really have time," and added, "Before, I used to read tons, but that was in elementary school. I guess I'm used to sort of not doing it anymore. I never get into it because I always feel like I have to be doing something [else]. I guess when I do have free time, I could read, but that's when I want to be with my friends."

Tracy regrets not doing community work, not learning in a way that she thinks makes most sense, and not reading out of school. When I ask other students, seniors, for example, if they could imagine, unTracy-like, doing less than they did, one told me that while "you can spend all your time on homework without any trouble," as he did, "you could also probably get by with a couple hours a night if you are willing to have a low C or D average." Another student, from the perspective of early June, with only graduation ceremonies and a hot summer between him and his first day of college, reflected on the possibility of working less intensely than he did, of taking more time to "just do other things, to go to the mountains. I'm just saying that metaphorically." He thought that there were students who did "go to the mountains," but they "are not going to the highest power, most rah-rah intense schools."

The cultural climate of Edgewood Academy creates and reinforces Tracy and the "rah-rah intense schools" aspirants in their internalized obligation to lead lives of frenetic activity. The Academy would be an insane place if all students were like them; it would not be what it is and means to be without them.

Whatever the particular configuration of demons that invades the students' souls, as a group they are subject to a set of overs: overextended, overworked, and overachieving. Academy students arguably entered the school already so afflicted. After all, they have not changed parents along the way to high school, and they did manage by the sixth grade to acquire those attributes that hoisted them over the admission barrier. "Parents are saying to me," a teacher explains, "we don't want them to work so hard. They're going to get an ulcer. They're working day and night. They're not sleeping enough." Teachers think this applies to about half the students. "I am fine, thank you," writes a student. "Actually, that is a preprogrammed response with which we've all been brainwashed. In reality, most of us are being pulled in three or four directions at the same time. Yesterday was the first day I had enough time to eat all three meals at a normal time. This is no problem, though, because I'm used to it."

I did not confirm either the teacher's "half" or the student's "most of us." What I heard repeatedly and uniformly was the students' expression of being overextended, which state their teachers and counselors confirmed. Displeased with the quality of his students' work, a teacher chided his students as "majors in overcommitment." He warned them that they could not use this condition as an excuse for poor work. Few Academy students would think to apologize for the extent of their involvement. To the contrary, "Students who don't overparticipate, who regularly go home after school, are thought weird." A senior student despairs of his personal overextendedness, of always feeling that whatever he does is at the expense of something else that he also has to be doing. This is normal. He still concludes, however, that "I think I'm better off, though, than if I was not being pulled like that." This, too, is normal. Being so pulled, he thought, was what was comfortable for him. "I just hope I don't get a stroke."

One student's overworked state is another's "managing nicely, thank you." It is uncool to claim to be underworked. Students learn that it is proper to claim always that they exist within inexhaustible layers of work and expectations from, say, their Russian teacher, their debate instructor, and their tennis coach, as if they were stars and these (faculty) others were claimants insisting on a piece of the action. Cool or otherwise, I am prepared to give credence to the student who writes:

> How am I? Well, with the little sleep I have I am so tired!! All the work can kill someone. What's the point of working us to death. I am so tired I don't think I can write anymore. I go home and work. WORK WORK WORK. Makes me angry. Work isn't always learning. It's boring very boring to have all the responsibilities!

I hear authentic sounds of overwork in this excerpt. It is from a young underclassman with several years experience with the Academy's pace and with learning how to manage time, make priorities, and develop strategies for surviving in an environment of excesses. Is he an overachiever, the last of the overs? I am not sure. This term originates in the talk of both teachers and students—a teacher tells me that "students in a school like this always come from families that are overachievers"—but it is a vague term. Another teacher called the Academy a "haven for overachievers, " a place where "students just do everything within their ability to do well and strive for those As and come in saying is there more I can do. And some students get a low A and that isn't even good enough. So there's this constant wanting to be the overachiever."

Does overachievement mean that students and their families and the faculty achieve more than by rights they ought to? For example, given students' talents, they should reach level X but, somehow, they succeed in reaching level Y, so that in some sense of excessiveness, they achieve more than they need to, and they want to achieve more than someone thinks they ought to. One teacher claims that overachievers are "real easy to identify. You know who they are by the second minute in your classroom. They are the ones who ask you three questions about what you just explained very clearly because they want to be sure they have it right so that they get every point. If there are going to be ten extra-credit points, they are going to want eleven."

The syndrome of overachievement includes being stressed, pressed for time, very, very hardworking, broadly participant, determined to succeed, and expectant of high grades and admission to the college of one's choice. This is the dominant view, the one that comes most readily to mind when Academy educators are invited to describe their students. It prevails at the same time that there is clear evidence that many students behave otherwise. The syndrome applies to a typical, not to an ideal, Academy student.

Perhaps my earliest sense of the Academy was that it is a place where stress is an ordinary attribute of life for students. A freshman boy says that in addition to all the normal "teenage peer pressures" of drinking, drugs, sex, romance—"all that stuff, you have the academic attitude instilled in you going to this school: you have to get good grades, you have to get your work done. It is not normal to twitch at 16 or cry at a C on a math test."

The school's stressful environment is sustained by teachers who are deeply disturbed when their students "glide by, and are not productive, committed members of the community." It is sustained by students who say about themselves that if "I put something off for a day, even though it's not due for another week, my stomach will start to turn. I am a guilty person; I am maimed by this disease." And also by a student who says that "This school somehow drains energy, emotion, excitement, confidence, and tolerance," but "I have no right to be complaining; I'm going to one of the best schools in the nation." An editorial that appeared in the Academy's student newspaper was entitled, "Students infected with unhappiness." The particular unhappiness the writer identified is "the sacrifice of high school present for college future."

GOODNESS

What is good about student goodness, I ask myself after having just discussed some of the costs to students. From what standpoint do I respond? Surely, the weight of American educational history would locate the source of such judgment making in the Academy's host community, notably with those parents who have chosen to send their children there. They affirm their satisfaction with the school's work, first, by enrolling their children; then, by keeping them there in the face of relatively high financial costs to themselves and psychological costs to their children; and, ultimately, by endorsing what the Academy does by means of their own motivation and pressure.

Goodness, as seen from the standpoint of students, embodies the inculcation and strengthening of cognitive skills, work habits, time-management skills, and attitudinal orientations to success that readies them to be off and running for forthcoming elite education, work, and lives. Students undergo an advantaging education, anticipating more advantage to come. Just how they define, seek, and gain advantage follows no single or predictable path. Attending Edgewood Academy raises the odds in their favor for attaining the advantage of choice future opportunities, those that embody relatively consequential position, power, and preference in American society.

The case for the Academy's contribution to advantage is hard to establish definitively, given other contributing factors, such as the ability of the students and the motivational insistence and modeling of their parents. Like the fate of good seeds in a garden tended by very expert gardeners, perhaps Academy students prosper and bloom in ways that defy measurement and beyond how they would fare in less expert hands, under less propitious educative conditions. What I do not doubt are the advantages that accrue to the students' sense of self by virtue of being admitted to the Academy and that contribute to their exceptional readiness for post-secondary academic success.

Lest it be thought that the school is like a high-powered, efficient educational assembly line, an Academy father can say about his children,

> I think our kids are treated very humanely. They have a good time. It's not just sticking them in classes and grinding them down, because I don't see kids who are ground down. My daughter gets up every morning at 5:45 so she can jump in the shower and get ready for school. She loves coming every day. She's a very social creature. The school has accommodated my son, who is an intellectual, and it's accommodated my daughter, who is not.

This father's view of his children is supported by even the most casual observation of the many different types of students who attend the school. To be sure, if the stringent admission requirements eliminate students who cannot survive the rigors of a demanding academic program, they do not thereby create any homogeneity of student interest and personality. Accordingly, diversity abounds, though it is contained within an untracked curriculum and a common frame of challenging academic standards. Like students everywhere, Academy students eventually learn where and how to locate themselves. The serious acting buffs learn one extant version of how to dress, where and with what peers and teachers to hang out, and what classes to take. The serious student of the social sciences or computers acquires similar knowledge. The serious athletes never doubt where to be and from whom to get support. As always, students create mini-environments for themselves, finding safe places to go to and safe people to be with, both young and old. In these places, they can comfortably promote their personal interests and skills in the company of like-minded others.

These environments do not threaten or undermine the college-prep overlay that powerfully orients teachers to offering Advanced Placement classes, to choosing particular textbooks, and to admonishing students to acquire this or that skill or understanding because it is what professors will expect of them. Upperclass teachers are not likely to overlook what is fixated in their students' lives. "Where, if at all, is the college factor in your daily life?" I ask a teacher. "The kids talk about it all the time." From another teacher I learn that her class is "like a college class. I don't feel inappropriate doing that [college-related learning] with my ninth graders. They need to learn how to do these things and the sooner they learn, the better. The more you get those skills, the better."

This latter teacher is not apologetic about what she does. Any regrets teachers have about what they do or feel compelled to do they attribute to the ascendancy of grades over learning. Teachers, and some students, bemoan the overemphasis on grades that leads, for example, to all U.S. History classes being Advanced Placement classes or to student obsession with their grades. Teachers know, and regret, that they too often can best reach students with the threat of a low grade, when they prefer to reach them with the enchantment of solving a problem, acquiring insight, mastering a poem, and the like. Older students know well that their academic passage is skewed toward what optimizes college success: "I was thinking most of my friends, and even myself, I mean, I don't really know if I have a dream anymore. If I can see past the next 2 years, which is just gonna be SAT, ACT, graduation, going to college, and, I mean, what's after that?"

What does goodness come down to? Certainly not to perfection—the perfect students, teachers, and outcomes. "I wish I didn't have to feel like I was in some sort of ivory tower," a student says. "And it hasn't been the perfect school, [but] what I've sacrificed has been much less than I've gained. And what I've gained has been really valuable." And from another student:

If I want to stay here, I'm going to put up with them preparing me, polishing me, for college. I'm going to have to put up with the grades. I'm going to have to sacrifice some sense of what I call my happiness so I can look at the world in a better way than if I'd gone to a public school. There's more pluses than minuses.

It is April, often a month of fine tidings for many senior students. It was for Dave Reston. I saw him before he saw me. We approached each other from opposite directions on the magnificent, tree-lined walk that connects the middle school and the high school. There was jubilance in Dave's step. As we drew closer to one another, I watched him lower and then raise his shaking hands high above his head, his fists clenched in the expression of triumph this move represents. When he saw me, he smiled and explained, "I got into Swarthmore."

6

Privilege

ABOUT PRIVILEGE

P*rivilege*, a versatile word, creates meaning as verb, noun, and adjective. My thinking about Edgewood Academy embraces all three forms of privilege. Generally, it is a valorizing term that relates to what its recipient perceives as beneficial.

The lives of Academy students bear strong resemblance to the lives students lead at elite universities and colleges and as employees in elite careers. Consider, for example, this picture of workers at Goldman, Sachs & Company, "the last big investment-banking partnership on Wall Street" (Cassidy, 1999, p. 28). They stay late, are expected to work without consideration for hours, and neglect their nonwork lives: "Workaholism is the norm, and so is constant pressure to perform. Every person in the firm is continually assessed ... The downside ... is that families, friends, and outside pursuits of any kind are neglected" (Cassidy, 1999, pp. 31–32). One might conclude that such companies had created the blueprint for the Academy's socializing experiences.

As some see it, privilege is obscene. It bears the stain of advantage and superiority that is unconscionable—"excessive, exorbitant, not guided or controlled by conscience, harsh, unjust" (Webster's, 1966)—and thus the heightened probability of its possessors attaining disproportionate opportunity, power, resources, and the like. So perceived, privilege leads to unfair outcomes of the type I recall hearing about as an adolescent who was directed to the evils of capitalism by the story of the rich man's dog that ate better than the poor man's child. Never mind that the rich man might have earned his wealth by means fully within the law, taking no unsavory shortcuts to his apex of pecuniary achievement. Never mind that the poor man never strived at school or on the job. The personal merit of the men struck me as beside the point in this matter of feeding dogs and children, or of offering health care, to cite another necessity too-often unequally available to animals and children.

Privilege, as I saw it in such instances, corrupts a rightful order, a moral order. The injustice in this simple image of my youth has never left me. In fact, poor children most certainly can and do attend Edgewood Academy. And poor children receive limited nutritional and medical benefits. Notwithstanding mitigating events, and the tale's adolescent simplicity, privilege rankles and gnaws at my sensibility; thereby do I acknowledge another major strand of my subjectivity.

Privilege can be categorized as either of the looking-down or the looking-up type. The former usually is of no account. Seldom do we find comfort in being comparatively better off than others; counting one's blessings has little currency. We do not often look down, or we look down no more than we need to, at those whose lives contrast negatively with our own, at those below us who could possibly look up and see us as privileged. If anything, it is the looking-up variety of privilege that disturbs us. It brings to mind those who have more or better of something that we value, and who, by virtue of the circumstances of their looked-up to-lives, are likely to continue to have more and better. The looking-up type of privilege is associated with choice country clubs, secluded vacation sites, and very expensive summer camps, restaurants, law firms, doctors, and, of course, schools. Access to these choice institutions typically requires financial means to an extent that makes them exclusive. Those looking up may understand that although holding privilege is not illegal, it feels wrong that it exists when their sense is of being left out, kept out, if not deprived.

I am more interested in privilege as it applies to circumstances and places about which almost anyone would say, "They bespeak of privilege." Or, as Paul Kingstown and Lionel Lewis (1990) conclude about elite schools in their book *The High-Status Track*, "their graduates are prepared for privilege and enjoy disproportionate access to high status occupations" (p. xi). When I invited Academy teachers to inform me about their school, I learned over and over that they view their school as a place of privilege. As one teacher reflected:

> For me, the school breaks down into two themes: the power of money and the power of intellect. When I feel great about being here, it is because I have a sense of authority because of my intellect. When I feel crappy, it seems that that power is worthless in the face of the other kind of authority.

Other teachers pick up on each of these themes. What this school is about, says one of the many teacher-administrators, is that if you can approach a problem or a topic or a concept in the right way, then you can get students to perform beyond your wildest expectation. ... The fact that we have people who can say, "I don't care if people say this can't be done, damn it, let's try, let's do this," maybe that, I guess, is at the heart of it.

This is the power of intellect! What this school is about, says another teacher, is "the self-definition of the elite, sort of the privilege, or the identity crisis of the privileged. If this is not a school for rich, White people anymore, which it hasn't been for a while, what exactly is it?"

PRIVILEGE AND GUILT

If you're going to write about the Academy and what makes it the Academy, you're going to have to think about the fact that it's so dang rich.
                                                              —*Academy teacher*

Being "so danged rich" does not ensure that one will act wisely as an educator. However, I'd gamble that great resources will induce more teacher inventiveness than scarce resources, which have not proved to be a surefire impetus to educational invention. Academy teachers have grounds to believe that they are cared for; Academy administrators have grounds to expect that Academy teachers will be devoted to their students. Being well paid will not put teachers on the side of angels; it should incline them more surely in that direction than otherwise.

Do you think that a place with an endowment of about $200,000,000, 300 acres, and the kind of facilities that we have isn't privilege? Of course, it's privilege! One of the manifest elements of a democratic, capitalistic society is that there are inequities.
                                                              —*Academy teacher*

Even with the changes that have been brought about in the school [those relating to bringing in many more financially aided students], the question is to what degree is it still an elitist institution? Do we serve simply to produce the next round of capitalists? The other day somebody used the term "whore of capitalism."
                                                              —*Academy teacher*

These two teachers testify to an awareness of the larger economic and political context of their school. Edgewood Academy as "whore of capitalism" is not my choice of metaphors for its characterization. "Whore" is a demeaning term. Its application outside of an occupational status connotes selling out, being up for grabs, a pawn to someone's bidding, and the moral worth of that someone deeply suspect. As an American school, the Academy educates on behalf of one or several versions of person, citizen, and worker in American society. All the versions incorporate an amalgam of democracy and capitalism as they have taken form at this time in our history. Agent of a society shaped by some extant expression of democracy and capitalism? Yes. Whore? No. More in the service of capitalism (in regard to profit, market forces, competition, individualism, and political, economic, and social inequities) than of democracy (in regard to freedoms, civil rights, the public good)? I incline toward the former, but I think I can examine the manifestations of privilege at the Academy without settling this question.

> I would be willing to believe, given that I think this is a faculty of conscience, that they would recognize and feel a little bit awkward about the abundance. We have so much. It's not embarrassment. I guess the [right] word is sort of an awkwardness.
>
> —*Academy teacher*

Awkwardness, embarrassment, even guilt—these were the sentiments I often heard when, following unsolicited remarks on this score, I explored the matter with teachers. None brushed the matter aside, though I think there may be a prevailing political correctness that disposes teachers to express some degree of unease at the Academy's affluence. Political correctness notwithstanding, I most often heard reasonably strong faculty reactions, well beyond the aforementioned teacher's awkwardness—his own educational upbringing was in a school like the Academy—and closer to embarrassment and guilt.

Writing about Mott, an expensive Quaker boarding school, Kim Hayes (1994) observed that "the school's exclusivity ... convinces pupils of their superiority" (p. 114). It is far more than the Academy's tuition costs that make it a privileged place. It is the considerable competition to gain admission. How not to feel superior in the face of the surmounting accomplishment of admission and the ensuing annual parade of student and teacher honors and achievements! Teachers believe that their students think, "I got in here and I deserve to be here," and this is not untrue. Given that the Academy rejects a majority of its applicants, the chosen few feel they justly deserve their chosenness. From chosenness to a sense of privilege is but one small step, with entitlement possibly following somewhere in the picture.

Day in and day out, however, students do not strut smugly about, exulting in their presence at the Academy; they have to attend to the demanding stuff of daily school life. To my researcher questions I most often heard both the critical and uncritical student gushingly conclude that being an Academy student was a matter of great good fortune. From being chosen to feeling privileged requires little more than experiencing the innumerable daily manifestations of Academy excellence. Feeling privileged is the norm.

We know best about something when we can see it in comparative perspective. Without comparisons, we cannot adequately locate ourselves, our lot, our fortune. Accordingly, when students are on campus with their fellows they do not "feel snobby," but when they are with public school friends, they are mindful of their difference: "You become ingrained with the idea [of difference], and the Academy perpetuates that. You are told constantly of how the Academy is ranked nationally, how your test scores rank against others. It just isn't healthy for a person to think they are great, even if they are." Another student graphically makes the point:

> Everyone thinks they're special because they go here. It's, like, when we take the SATs. There's a lot of different rooms. I was in a little room and there was, like, five Academy students. We had this air about ourselves like SAT is no big deal. All the Academy kids are going, like, "Hey, no problem."

> I don't like it when I feel superior, but it's, like, that's what it's all about. Like you're going to be better off than all these other public school kids [who are there taking the same examination and feeling that it is a problem]. Since you go to the Academy, you'll be better off at college because you'll be better prepared. You'll be better prepared for life. You'll get the better job. You'll be better, you're the better, you're the best. The Academy is the best!

> Is it more capitalist, though, that you're trying to be better than anyone else? That's the whole idea about it that our parents want us to achieve out in the world, which is a capitalist society, right? They want us to be the haves, not the have nots, because, of course, the haves take advantage of the have nots. Of course, they want to send us here so we can have all the tools.

Capitalism, again, if only in the voice of a sardonic student who reflects what he knows are his parents' reasons for sending him to the Academy. Students, parents, and teachers do not ordinarily speak the language of haves and have nots, though such thinking is inevitably there. To be sure, parental motives for sending their children to the Academy do not exclude getting a sound education. They also favor its relative physical safety compared to public schools, and its personal safety, as in the case of the student who explained that, "My parents, I think they were worried about my personality traits. They knew that, you know, maybe if I got into the public schools that I would, you know, go into the wrong scene." Her parents are right; there are no wrong crowds or scenes at the Academy of the type that can be found in many public schools and that her parents feared would lead her astray. Notwithstanding a range of parental motivations, it is the advantage an Academy education confers that is primary, and it is relative advantage vis-à-vis other American teachers and students that underlies whatever feeling of unease teachers feel.

As a high school teacher, I felt guilty when I failed to return student examinations as soon as I had promised, when I was less prepared than I thought I ought to be, or when, too often, I was less patient and understanding than I needed to be. Never did it occur to me to feel the least twinge of guilt because of where I had been offered employment or of my working conditions, even though by comparison with many school districts I was fortunate in my suburban Chicago location.

Teachers from public school backgrounds, whose families were of relatively modest economic means, may speak somewhat fancifully of their sense of being at the Academy:

> When I came here it was kind of like, you know, how you would walk into a palace. I picture myself, if I were to walk into the Buckingham Palace, I would tiptoe. Oh, this is so plush. I can picture many teachers having that feeling coming into this environment.

Another such teacher, agitated by our discussion of the place of schools like the Academy in American society, told me, "You are in an area that I am not comfortable in and you know it! I am not a private school person. Private schools serve a function … that you can't get otherwise in mainstream public schools. But I sure have a hard time justifying it." In fact, I did not know she was uncomfortable, having failed to interpret all the things she had been telling me as indicators of someone who, while happy with her job, nonetheless held a conception of herself as educator of the people, not of the select. For her and others who knew first-hand the life of a public school teacher, it was just too good and too easy to teach such bright, well behaved students, and to be so well-paid for doing so under luxurious conditions.

Teachers who had attended private schools spoke of their unease in other terms. "It has taken me decades to get to the point to say, 'I teach at a very wealthy school,'" remarked a teacher who relished his freedom to teach as he wished. What worried him about the Academy was "obscenity in wealth," because, he added, money, like weapons of war, could reach a point where it becomes obscene. This man of conscience was struck by his school's sense of excess, compared to what most schools elsewhere possess. Neither he nor anyone else I met wanted to moderate this educational bounty, though teachers never dismissed the question that, eventually, I asked: Did there need to be schools like the Academy? Yes, they answered, often speaking circularly, because students like theirs needed schools like the Academy if educational justice is to be done to the students. By the time I incorporated this question into my interview portfolio, I had heard enough to feel assured that I was not introducing an issue that was alien to teacher considerations, not least after the day a teacher volunteered that "the democrat in me has trouble being at this school."

This "democrat in me" continues his observations:

> I think I mentioned a while back a phrase of becoming a whore of capitalism. I mentioned that phrase because we are a school that plays a certain part in a class structure that sends people to influential [postsecondary] schools and positions of power. You can't deny that. Is it possible to teach in a place like this, knowing that is true? Again, not deny it, but not become driven by it? That has been a struggle for me and, I know, for a lot of people, not just in my department.

Again, the language of class and capitalism. Though not everyone's framework for thinking about the Academy, this teacher's "struggle," as he puts it, presents intensely what to some degree is the concern of many of the faculty.

"Guilty privilege" (Kaminsky, 1992, p. 41) aptly captures the sense of those whose unease with the Academy resides in the unresolved tension between what they believe a democratic society ought to be like and the prevalence of privilege in that society. More specifically, the unease derives from the persistence of equality as an ideal of democracy, and the seemingly irreconcilable relationship between privilege and equality.

If few people ever think of equality, strictly taken, as a practical or realizable ideal, many may still take issue with degrees and forms of inequality. Unequal access to spas, country clubs, and Concorde flights embody disparities of slight consequence to most people. When, however, the disparity relates to strikingly differential educational advantage, then the consequences are of national import. They reside in inequalities of educational opportunity whose resolution is bogged in underfunded, underimagined responses. However, given the proliferation of public and private alternatives of educational choice, one is hard put to know what means and ends of schooling would represent acceptable equal opportunity. Personal tastes and insecurities conspire with legislative bandwagons to sustain this proliferation, leaving one to conclude that "I can't define educational justice, but I know educational injustice when I see it."

PRIVILEGE AND ITS CONSEQUENCES

For some time, elite institutions have been unwilling or unable to sustain the exclusivity that historically accompanied their eliteness. In the case of Edgewood Academy, the democratization of admissions began with Mr. Compton's predecessor, Arthur Bradford, who supported the acceptance of minority students in proportion to their percentages in the surrounding community. In an audiotaped interview prepared for the school's archives, he acknowledged that there was "a relatively small number of candidates each year [who] come from families where there is indeed a financial need." Nonetheless, he added, "we should not beat the bushes" to find poor but academically qualified students, recalling that the eager efforts of several of his faculty to recruit Black students failed. It would take the appointment of Mr. Compton, as headmaster, and Mr. Garcia, as Assistant Director of Admission, to vigorously pursue the recruitment of poor and minority students before the complexion—and exclusivity—of the Academy would change. The Academy was not alone in this change. By 1991, over a period of 20 years, "students of color" in the approximately 1500 independent schools across the nation had increased from 5% to an average of 13% (Kane, 1991, p. 403; see also Powell, 1996, who estimates that the increase may be as high as 28% [1996, pp. 98–99, 271–272]).

By whatever name, this move among institutions of all types has changed forever who participates in them, the exclusivity of schools like the Academy more notably a matter of academic criteria than of family and fortune. The Academy's numbers are impressive. In the 1991-1992 academic year, of about 900 students in Grades 6 through 12, 623 paid the full tuition of $6,250; 301, or 32%, received aid. The average grant was $3,800. In the years thereafter, no fewer than 30% of all Academy students received financial aid, and no fewer than 30% of all students were "students of color." This occurred even as the overall student enrollment had expanded by 1998 to just over 1000 and the number of applicants compared to the number accepted had expanded by a factor of three or four, depending on the year. These figures cannot reveal the enormous investment of energy and concern by Mr. Garcia and others to attract students to a school that even some years after Mr. Compton had arrived was still not readily seen as a school "for the likes of us." Here is Mr. Garcia speaking to this point:

> There is almost total ignorance about this school. Last spring, to give you an idea, I went to an elementary school [located across town from Edgewood Academy] to speak to fifth graders. There was not one child out of forty that knew about the Academy. They thought it was a police school, a military school. For those who at least had heard about it, it was still that school for the rich and they could not think they could come here.

That such children have come to the Academy is the result of a commitment to diversity and a policy of generous financial aid (1.2 million in 1991 and 2.4 million by 1997). This success is a primary point of Academy pride. It is the single most-cited accomplishment that Academy educators believe mitigates their privileged status. This success represents the extension of advantage to young men and women who ordinarily might not even have aspired to attend a school like Edgewood Academy. Sometimes mentioned was the advantage to Academy students of the enriching perspectives provided by the newcomers whose presence financial aid made possible.

Elite schools often associate the fact of advantage with the activity of giving back. Edgewood Academy's pursuit of excellence does not embrace a robust curricular investment in such activity, but giving back was a matter of concern that surfaced when I directed teacher attention to their school as a privileged institution. For their part, teachers were somewhat active in churches, synagogues, and service organizations; I did not pursue this matter, thinking that teaching, particularly as typically performed at the Academy, is itself a substantial expression of giving back. One teacher volunteered, "How, in good conscience, you know, can you not stay in touch with the common good? How can you not turn around and go, 'God, if I don't in some way make a contribution outside of the school … '" Her zeal, as directed to the out-of-school activity of teachers, is uncommon, but not as it applies to students and their commitment to the common good.

Conventional Academy belief was that their students should be civic-minded, oriented to the public good, an ideal worthy in its own right for everyone, but all the more so for Academy students, the teachers argued, given their advantages. The school carefully avoided any hint of noblesse oblige. Teachers were more comfortable with a sort of trickle-down view of giving back: provide an outstanding education to the students, who then are prepared to contribute to society through whatever jobs and careers they come to have. Debate at the Academy about giving back, such as it was, centered on whether to require community service or leave it optional and thus a matter that currently involved under 10% of Academy students.[1] An Academy teacher who is actively involved in the school's service organization identifies service work as just an undercurrent at the school "that people tune out." The regularly involved students are available when they are needed. Otherwise, they are "more ignored [by other students] than anything."

---

[1]On this point of students from elite schools giving back, Nicolas Lemann (1997) writes,

According to the original design, the American meritocracy was supposed to function like Plato's Republic: the best students would be found and given elaborate special training … [but] they don't do with their lives what they [are] supposed to [that is, run the State] … they're an elite that lacks legitimacy. … They … are too obviously self-interested to have an automatic high moral standing with the public. (p. 33)

See also Lukas (1998) on the decline of codes of responsibility among the elite. On the state of American youth in general, Glendon (1991) reports on the results of the 1990 Times Mirror Center survey that found that "the current cohort [of young people] knows less, cares less, votes less, and is less critical of its leaders and institutions than young people have been at any time over the past five decades" (p. 129). This confirms the 1989 findings of a People for the American Way survey that "'Young people have learned only half of America's story … [they] emphasize freedom and license almost to the exclusion of service or participation'" (reported in Glendon, 1991, p. 128). This finding may always have been true (see Educational Policies Commission, 1963).

Two different teachers made related observations. One vacillated on whether he thought his students had bought into the concept of a common good, eventually concluding that, although "certainly curious about it," they had not. How could they, given, as was his impression, that a narrowly, self-oriented individualism had triumphed in the country over the common good, so that "the kids, when you say, buy into it, I think it's more they're not sure what "it" is. Where would they get their knowledge of it?" The other teacher complimented students who help special needs kids learn to ski, tutor elementary school students, and paint hospital walls, but he yearned to have discussions with students that would begin with them saying, "'It will be important to me when I pick a job that my job have to do with improving human welfare in one way or another.' They're not very interested in having that conversation." And he also wanted students to know the difference between charity and justice.

The teachers identify significant issues. The first one places what does not happen to Academy students in the context of what does not prevail in the larger society. Can schools make even a dent in advancing something as fundamental as what Dewey called an "organized, articulate Public" (Dewey, 1927), when there is not such a "Public" beyond the school whose values and behavior can be built on and reinforced? If Edgewood Academy experiences no resistance to its efforts in this regard, it also has no constituency for such work that would make it competitive in any way with its prep-school thrust.

Nor, indeed, is there much of a constituency for Academy students learning to grasp, let alone to grapple with, the charity–justice distinction that the second teacher embraced. The cognitive and affective underpinnings of an act are not necessarily discernible from the act itself, but there is a profound difference regarding one's engagement with the common good if one is moved by *charity*—doing good, rather than by *justice*—doing right.

A few years ago, two media-drenched stories relating to privilege became front-page news. The first and larger of the two, the O. J. Simpson trial, involved a former football hero and TV celebrity accused of killing his wife and her friend. He was defended by a platoon of legal experts. We saw them in their courtroom setting, participants in a grizzly drama. The public learned about the financial cost to Simpson of this cadre of defenders. The case would diminish neither their fame nor their fees. It is their fees that catch my attention. Privileged by his wealth, Simpson could extend his personal advantage into the realm of the legal system: when he appeared in the courtroom, he was not just one more accused man. When Simpson stood before judge and jury, arguments of guilt had large walls to scale; defenses sprang up to parry each prosecution thrust. Thus does advantage operate in the legal system.

The second case involved former baseball star Mickey Mantle and his life-and-death search for a liver transplant at a time of "desperate shortage" of livers. His story always was that of the New York Yankees great who as an alcoholic abused his liver for 40 years. His defenders said his fame would not give him precedence over anyone else in acquiring a liver. He would take his place on the list fashioned by criteria of need, tissue matching, circumstance, and so on, that apply equally to everyone. That said, Mantle received a transplant within 2 weeks and the cries of "foul" and "queue jumping" began. Thus is advantage presumed to operate in the medical system.

What different instances of privilege share is advantage—at the expense of others in the medical case where there is a painfully finite supply of livers, and relative to others in the legal and educational case. Given an infinite supply of justice, Simpson can be acquitted without necessarily doing damage to anyone else's interest, but it can be argued that his case engenders a cynicism that undermines the legal system. Although there is a finite supply of privileged education, limited by location, cost, and the academic qualifications of student applicants, more and other schools, unlike organs, always are available, albeit not schools like the Academy. However, those whom the Academy admits do not thereby deprive anyone else of access to schooling, except at the Academy, which has a fixed number of openings for each class.

The advantage that privilege affords is sometimes part of a zero-sum case—if I win, you cannot. The cost is very high to those who fail to get a liver, kidney, or lung. Schooling is not a zero-sum game, not least because of the role that taste or preference plays in the decision of schooling for one's children. Not only is there an array of types of nonpublic schools, there also is increasing choice within public schools. Parents seek the "advantages" they think are available from a particular type of school, for example, one that features religion or a back-to-the-basics curriculum or foreign language immersion.

When I was about ready to complete my data collection at the Academy, I asked students and teachers what they thought my book ought to be about. One teacher said that it should be about the "identity crisis of the privileged." At very few schools in this country could I have received such an answer. It is not an answer that suits everyone at the school. For example, after months of interviewing students and teachers about all aspects of their school, including their reactions to being in such a well-endowed school, I was unprepared for the defensive response of a teacher who felt he was under attack:

> *T:* You have to be careful, if I might say so [he advised me]. You are coming in looking at the school with this notion of privilege. I'd really be careful.

> *AP:* I didn't come in looking for it. I didn't come in even thinking that. It never occurred to me before.
>
> *T:* Oh.
>
> *AP:* It's just a privilege being here.
>
> *T:* Oh, really! Why do you think I'm privileged?

I explained that I thought the term was justified by the quality of the students, his colleagues, the physical facilities—all the things that I have been writing about, including having a string quartet in residence.

> *T:* Are you saying because the American public school system is in shambles that you shouldn't have anybody who's trying to do something better, independently of that system? You see, I think the implications of what you say are really dangerous.
>
> *AP:* I'm not saying any of that.
>
> *T:* That's the flip side of what you're saying.

In strong contrast are teachers who speak of tension between democracy and privilege, saying—guilt, once again—that it is something they have "spent time feeling badly about. I can't apologize for where I've come from, but there it is. What I can do is just make the most of it. There is responsibility. I don't think there's any denying that."

On the matter of responsibility, I asked students to speculate if they did not enter the Academy with a commitment to community service, to some form of giving back, would they likely leave with such a commitment. Junior and senior students, all of them having been at the Academy since the sixth grade, were of several minds, as exemplified here:

It's definitely not required that we do community service. A lot of kids participate in it. I have from time to time. Certainly in history class we talk about politics and getting involved with what's going on outside of this school. We should be able to take what we've learned here and apply it to other people, to benefit other people, which I'm not sure if we're really encouraged to do. ... If you weren't interested in community service, you could easily get away with doing nothing. I think you could easily leave not thinking it was really important. It would be kind of hard not to [she adds, as if by afterthought] just because there is so much community service going on all the time.

Up until about 2 years ago they didn't even, you know, it was kind of, like, yeah, it's a nice school. You are pretty rich. Go to school, go to class. Now it's becoming more, like, yes, well, you do owe something. ... Of late at the school I've seen that attitude amongst the students and I can't imagine that that's not encouraged by the faculty.

The people who do participate in the community don't do it out of any sense of obligation. It makes them feel good. That's the feeling I get. I think there is not a very large feeling in our class that we have an obligation to give anything back. I think there is a very large feeling we need to show our gratitude to the Academy by acquiring for ourselves as much as we possibly can. It's less about community service than self-service. In strict community service things, it's the same group of people who always do it. There is hardly any talk in any of our classes about our obligation to do something, either by faculty or by students. I really can't think of a time that it was ever really an issue that we needed to help those less fortunate.

Gary Simons (1992) concluded an article he wrote several years ago with the indisputable thought that "Developing a compassionate awareness of the life circumstances of others in privileged young people and motivating them to further the common good would ennoble a school's mission" (p. 274). I believe this, too. But rereading Simons's (1992) final lines has made me rethink one aspect of this matter: "Given the advantages independent schools have over their public school counterparts," he wrote, "if we cannot expect an independent school to incorporate these ... purposes as an integral part of their missions, what possibility is there that America can be 'the last, best hope of mankind?'" (p. 274).[2] I don't like Simons's "last, best hope" expectation. And I resist concluding that students at these schools, or at any others in the vast middle between those at the desperate and those at the advantaged ends, should be held to different, lesser standards for responsibility to the common good. All schools everywhere should be held to such standards, their students assumed to be as capable of grasping the necessity of compassionate awareness and the common good as any other students. These understandings may be very difficult to develop, but they are neither esoteric nor obscure.

One might think that elite schools can more readily implement the goal of good works. Perhaps they can. Guilt, good sense, and motivating circumstance may be differentially distributed among students in elite and nonelite schools. I don't believe anyone knows about this with any certainty. Nonetheless, it seems obvious that everyone can and should learn, for example, that we all suffer in a world that defines the profligacy of the buccaneer individualist as "success"; that the recourse to social problems with avoidance, denial, and invisibility is a sure

---

[2]In his review of Kingston and Lewis's book *The High Status Track* (1990), Marvin Bresler (1991) wrote that "we are reduced to the innocent hope that elite schools will develop in their students the competencies and commitments that predispose them to surrender to the constraints of moral principle" (p. 868).

path to their festering; and that we need to acquire what Bellah, Sullivan, Sundler, and Tipton (1985) called "effective sympathy" (p. 251, and see all of their chapter 10, The National Society), and what Rorty (1989) described as "the imaginative ability to see strange people as fellow sufferers" (p. xv).

We should not expect only those who have attended elite schools to be informed about and experienced with decisions relating, for example, to architectural conservation, the development of new housing projects, the design of a city's public buildings, the level of the minimum wage, the provision of city parks and green belts, the zoning allowances for advertising signs, the ethical dilemmas of spotted owls versus jobs for lumberers, and the responsibility of industry for pension security and plant closings. "One learns," explains Bellah et al. (1991), "not through accumulating tested propositions about the objective world, but through participation in social practices, by assuming social roles … One becomes what one knows" (p. 158). The specific point here is about citizenship.

The general point is about expectation. It is self-serving for those within the elite-school fold to argue for expecting more from their students, relative to students elsewhere, because they are so privileged. This reinforces the chosenness–distinctiveness status of everyone in these schools, the setting-apart-from-others sense that already is entrenched in the structure of these schools. I would prefer that the argument for good citizenship be made on the grounds of the essential civic responsibility of all students, rather than on the grounds of privilege. To do so would increase the probability of justice rather than charity being an operative principle. Still, if elite schools can successfully motivate their students to make a privilege-responsibility association, they may possess more than a good starting point for grasping the idea of justice.

There is, regrettably, evidence that when schools undertake pedagogical activity that relates to the common good, they raise the specter of trespassing on the protective sensibilities of parents and community groups. For example, take the case of Washington State. It "dropped a controversial goal that asked students to demonstrate that they would be responsible and caring individuals in society" (Olson, 1993, p. 26). What seemed a "motherhood and apple pie" recommendation was anything but. The antagonism of the Christian Coalition and the Eagle Forum, to name just two such groups, to educational practice that extends beyond what they think is "safe" and "basic" gives independent schools a clear view of what they are relatively independent of. Moreover, it gives all of us a clear awareness that there may be no motherhood and apple pie-type recommendations that can be made for education. Nonetheless, I look at the advantages that accrue to Edgewood Academy students and conclude that it is in our collective self-interest that advantage be optimized for all American children.

Privilege and advantage, guilt and giving back, individualism and the common good—these are matters about schooling that the experience of Edgewood Academy highlights. They are not the stuff of Monday morning when classes want teaching, but of what schools are about in their inescapably broader terms. And it is to the broader terms of American values that are manifest in Edgewood Academy that I turn next.

American Values

INTRODUCTION

Asociety's values are manifest in the settings and circumstances of its institutions and organizations where the business of its people is conducted. We gain access to different perspectives depending on our focal point. Consider what can be learned about values by exploring, for example, the workings of the military, the welfare establishment, corporations, retirement homes, and transportation systems—to take a disparate lot by way of illustration. We learn something important and different from each of these vantage points. What each reveals is partial, overlapping, and sometimes at odds with what we might learn from the others. My window to American Values is through schools and what happens to children in them. More specifically, I reflect here on the ramifications of elite schools.

In what follows, I restate the framework within which I have been writing. I have taken a moral perspective because it highlights an abiding fact about schools: They mean to affect student behavior in ways that are consequential for their lives. Thus, what they do, accordingly, is engage daily and invariably in moral decisions and moral actions, notwithstanding that they would not necessarily label their decisions and actions as moral. Of course, it is more normal, more descriptive to identify what happens in schools as teaching and learning. To think of teaching and learning as not just implicated but replete with moral consequences is to be readied for considering Edgewood Academy and the images it presents of American Values. This consideration is the substance of my response to the question I raised in chapter 1 about the outcome of this research: What can I learn from studying Edgewood Academy that transcends the particular case of this school? I come to that discussion in a moment. For now I will note that what I have learned brings to mind the sense of schooling I got from several years of learning about adolescents in a rural school in central Illinois. *Growing Up American* (Peshkin, 1978/1994) is the title of that study, an apt one, I thought, for its identification of village Mansfield's children acquiring one of the many extant ways of growing up as an American. In the case of Edgewood Academy, I see another way of growing up American, one no less American for all its differences from rural Mansfield. The force of its students' compelling advantage draws me to the half-empty cup of what other children in America do not have.

I begin with a brief picture of a set of values that resonate in the Academy experience. They attach to the school overall, that is, to the norms, practices, and behavior of educators and students. Several of them—pursuit of excellence and change-oriented—are explicit, contained in the thrust of the headmaster's leadership. Several of them seem naturally to accompany these explicit values—industriousness and progressiveness. I identify this set of values as central in the development of students growing up American—Academy style. Overall, their old-fashioned ring suggests the advice offered to young men of the 19th century who yearned to get ahead.

Over several years of association with the Academy, I have been struck by its exemplification of devoted, wise leadership and teaching, and also of decency and industriousness, the latter a very American attribute. These qualities are not the outcome of money; clearly, all that is good at the Academy does not result from its wealth. The confluence of dedicated, striving educators, parents, and students makes for a school that others can learn from. However, what many observers of the Academy experience could well carry away is a sadness at the impossibility of carrying anything away because of the school's exceptionality: for one thing, the selection factor that operates with regard to educators and students, and, for another, the school's enormous resources. If onlookers are deterred by what they believe the Academy possesses, they should look again at the Academy's industriousness. Everyone there works hard. What personal talents its participants possess are enhanced by their determined, persistent effort over time. As a nation, we celebrate industry.

And it is not industry for its own sake, but in pursuit of excellence, the much-touted, much-aspired quality for all that it does. The Academy's garnering of educational capital may, indeed, arouse envy, but we do not fault schools for their plenty, for their realization of the American Value of money honestly acquired and put to good educational use. More than this, the Academy's virtue is secured by its serious pursuit of excellence, which, like the astronaut's "right stuff," is a most respected value, one that most schools perhaps honor more in the breech, but honor nonetheless. The Academy testifies to excellence in word and deed. "We do things because we think it is right," says an Academy administrator and teacher, "not because we have to. I respect us for that. I like that we pursue excellence." If I question some of what accompanies the school's drive for excellence—prizes, trophies, stress, unbalanced lives, and more—I do not doubt the industriousness of its participants.

This lineup of American Values contains one that Academy educators repeatedly emphasized. All year, I had attended meetings and heard talk about the changes planned for the next 5 years. I did not immediately appreciate a fundamental fact. As a relatively new school, unencumbered by a hallowed, ivied tradition, teachers and administrators believed that they were free to entertain change to a commendable degree:

> I think that provides us with the opportunity to establish, as perhaps a principal tradition here, institutional self-examination in a very serious way. You will consciously pick up every stone in the place and decide where you are going to put it back, or whether you can discover a more perfect place. This gives us the chance to do some great things in education.

In short, as this Academy teacher articulates, an orientation to change is an abiding state of mind at the Academy, one that inclines the school's educators to be disposed to reflect, reconsider, and change in the interest of doing better than they already do.

The interplay of industriousness, a commitment to excellence, and a basic orientation to change adds up to establishing at the Academy what the late sociologist James Coleman (1988) called "social capital ... the norms, the social networks, the relationships between adults and children that are of value for the children's growing up" (p. 12). A school's contribution of "opportunities and demands" joins the family's and community's contribution of "attitudes and effort" to produce fertile conditions for the academic success of children (Coleman, 1988, pp. 10–14). Academy students may reap benefits from both school and home; if their home is lacking, however, they can obtain supportive "attitudes and effort" from the school's adults and student peers.

Academy educators and students are aristocrats of educational opportunity. They can transcend the quotidian prospects of even the best of the local public schools, their own pedagogical trove a tower of excess, by comparison. From another perspective, it is no less than all children deserve. If such academically accomplished, nonpublic schools weren't already fully legal entities, their justification might be found in their city-on-a-hill promise, in their capacity to demonstrate what is possible. I see them as among our educational Joneses with whom it would pay to stay abreast, less in the particulars of their educational offerings than in their amplitude. The educational preferences of Americans are too idiosyncratic to safely generalize about them; it is much safer to generalize about the universal appeal of amplitude, about creating schools under circumstances of material and pedagogical plenty.

"Progressive" is a word not much used nowadays to describe either individuals or institutions. It aptly describes the Academy. Accordingly, Academy graduates take away with them a dedication to progress, a quality that has been a centerpiece of American rhetoric throughout its history. As a nation, we believe in progress, that things can and will get better, that clouds have silver linings, sometimes gold. Confidence, optimism, and hope resonate throughout the school, from the performances on its numerous tennis courts, to those in its well-stocked laboratories, its swank library, and its several computer rooms. And more and more and more. Academy progressiveness is manifest in its lawns and landscape, its old and new buildings, the quality of each year's applicants, the number of Advanced Placement classes taken and passed, ad infinitum: Academy things and people, by some measure, get better and better.

I continue with an excerpt from the report of an externally-led evaluation team that was composed of several outsiders and several Academy educators. They evaluated the school's history department. Over time, each subject matter area of the school is assessed for accreditation purposes by the school's professional association. The team spent many long, full days in intensive interviewing of students and teachers, observing classes, and examining relevant documents. What they wrote under "Commendations" will sound much like what I have written elsewhere:

> The History Department at the Academy is in the enviable situation of having at its disposal remarkable resources in terms of classroom facilities, technologies, library, and development funds, so that both at the level of curriculum innovation and multimodal classroom learning and at the level of faculty enrichment it is possible to pursue *any* worthwhile experiment without encumbrance or delay.

I added emphasis to "any" because it is the emblem of educational privilege. How incredible that such an observation could be made about any school! It contrasts strikingly with the decision the State of Illinois Appellate Court made in the case of Louis E. v. Joseph A. Spagnolo: "states and local school districts have a constitutional obligation to provide a *minimally* (my emphasis, once more) safe and adequate public education to their students" (State Must Run Adequate Public Schools, 1997, p. 2). By looking down, the American Civil Liberties Union could celebrate these findings, seeing in them prospects for improving the East St. Louis schools that Kozol (1991) studied (see his *Savage Inequalities*), whose "faulty fire alarms" and "outdated textbooks," to say the least, were the basis for the lawsuit. By looking up, I see the persistence of enormous disparity, a forthcoming better for desperately straitened schools, but a better that is weepingly distant from a best, however conceptualized, which all children deserve. The discrepancy between my italicized "any" and "minimally" dramatizes the disparity of access to educational advantage in American society. My concern for this gap parallels my awe at the Academy's educational marvels as an aspect of my subjectivity.

An Academy teacher expresses the school's operative circumstance: "Not very many people have access to what we have access to here. In the whole world, you don't have this." Academy students benefit from an ongoing success-begetting process. They are achievement winners in a sort of national contest wherein, relatively speaking, there are numerous achievement losers. In a state, nation, and world "of the haves and have nots," as an administrator observed, "these kids just happen to be among the haves." It is this fact, this signifier of educational injustice, that shapes my perception of the larger meaning of Edgewood Academy.

In its own terms, I find much to admire in what the Academy offers. In terms of the gap, I find much to despair of. The advantages of elite schools engender inequalities of life chances and sustain not just distant but virtually parallel worlds. The people in these worlds exist for each other most often as abstractions and statistics, as caricatures and stereotypes.

AMERICAN VALUES

Briefly, these values compose a generally coherent picture, beginning with *Personal School Choice*. By this value, individuals have the right to reject their designated public school in favor of a nonpublic school that for some reason pleases them more. What Americans do not have is the right to be granted admission to the school of their choice. This is the implication of the second value—*Institutional Student Choice*. By this value, institutions have the prerogative to determine who and on what basis they will admit those who seek enrollment. *Extending the American Dream* is the third value, by means of which many poor students are brought to the prospects of good fortune, of getting ahead, possibly to an extent beyond anything they could have imagined. Once students are admitted to nonpublic schools they are subject to the fourth American Value—*Institutional Advantaging*. By this value, nonpublic schools exercise their right to "stamp" their students with the peculiar attributes, for example, of religion, ethnicity, skills, or academic achievement, that are embedded in their raison d'etre. I think of the Academy's stamp as a mobility passage resulting in social differentials that further hierarchical distinctions in American society. We do not so much value hierarchy as we accept it as a natural outcome of human variation. However, what outcomes we accept or reject relate to the last point—*Permissible Advantage*, which is both an American Value and the conclusion to this section. It deals with the fact that as a society we construe some inequalities of advantage as acceptable, while rejecting others.

Personal School Choice

The Academy signifies a most cherished American Value—school choice. State laws require children to attend school; they do not demand that all children attend the same type of school. For every American child there is a designated public school somewhere that their place of residence dictates they may attend. Though no child is outside this arrangement, it is avoidable. Nonpublic schools are the means to this avoidance.

The most basic fact about every type of nonpublic school is that each is grounded in perceptions of discontent with or of unavailable opportunity in a particular public school or all public schools. The discontent may be located in public school attributes and outcomes that relate to some or all of these factors: its underlying philosophy of education; who does or does not attend; who teaches; what is and is not taught; what is and is not emphasized within what is taught; and what rules and regulations govern the school. Put another way, every type of nonpublic school embodies some conception of advantage, compared to one's designated public school, that is the reason for choosing it.

I rejected nonpublic schools the first time I encountered them as a new high school teacher when four of my best students left their fairly high aspiring, rich suburban school to attend private, boarding high schools. I was disappointed, I thought they had made a mistake, and I did not understand why they left. As I saw them, public schools were an integral part of American democracy and my students belonged in them. Nonpublic schools were not, their advantaging capabilities then no part of my understanding.[1] My childhood experience with nonpublic schools was confined to parochial schools, and they struck me as suspect, separatist institutions with good football teams.

---

[1]In this respect, educator Deborah Meier (1995) wrote, "Neither equity, civil rights, nor mutual respect for the ideas of others are always the winners even in public institutions—far from it—but public schooling shifts the odds in favor of such democratic principles" (p. 36). Neither Meier nor I write in the spirit of the benefactors, the CEO Foundation, who gave an entire community in Texas the option to send their children to private schools: "its leaders say it wants to show how free-market forces in education will improve a monopolistic public system" (Walsh, 1999, p. 50).

I have never thought I should modify my views about the public school-democracy connection. I have come to understand, however, that if respect for cultural difference is to be authentic and not nominal, families must have educational choice. Moreover, the values of liberty and individualism further deny the hegemony of one type of school over all others. These values argue for different types of schools being available to satisfy different personal tastes. Still, I resist thinking that public money should be made available to any nonpublic school. This ostensible contradiction rests on the simultaneity of respect I feel for the idea of schools that serve and support difference, and the even stronger respect I feel for our public schools. In them, I see differences being manifest naturally (and imperfectly), albeit never always and as fully as is necessary to show proper regard for existing cultural variability in our society.

Nonpublic schools are born in difference of some type—for example, in religious doctrine, social class behavior, academic standards, pedagogical philosophy, ethnicity—that individuals and groups believe cannot be honored in, perhaps even is threatened by, their local public school, possibly in all public schools located anywhere. Nonpublic schools reflect someone's consideration that public schools are limited in ways that preclude their serving as proper, decent, safe, or adequate places to educate children.

In this country, the nonpublic school has a long tradition, harking back to the time when churches more often than legislatures were committed to educating children. The ultimate nonpublic school for enshrining personal choice is the home school (see Sandham, 1998). In such schools, the parent cum teacher can make all the decisions about what knowledge is central, and what is peripheral; about what constitutes a good person; and about how to learn and how to use what is learned. As a nation, we are becoming accustomed to what once appeared to be the desperate measures of parents to ensure their children's physical, emotional, spiritual, and cognitive well-being. It took a while for state school officials to learn how to respond to home schools. It may take them longer to know how to respond to the school that a coven of witches in Concord, California, planned to open with the help of vouchers, if the voucher initiative had passed. The proposed school's curriculum would have included spell-casting and potion-making.

> Sean Walsh, a spokesman for the Choice in Education League … said that the witches probably would not be able to open a school because they would fail background checks or provisions that outlaw schools permitting "unlawful" behavior. (Pagans Want Vouchers for a Witchcraft School, 1993, p. A5)

What is honored generally by the very existence of nonpublic schools is the American Value of educational choice. The underlying ideal of this value says, in effect, that although significant expressions of diversity are lost when smart or religious or ethnic students are not present in their local public school, something of fundamental importance would be lost if all children were compelled to attend their local public school. What nonpublic schools honor specifically is the opportunity to perpetuate or replace certain cultural norms in order to establish or crystallize other cultural norms. At the Academy, the cultural norms relate to elite personal advantage.

Nonpublic schools are born in and epitomize difference that sets them apart from the schools that most children attend. This is grounds for celebration for some, but grounds for unease for others who do not want uniformity in their public schools but value them as the seedbeds of democracy that accommodate everyone. Barring severe disability, they must erect no barriers to admission. What does it say about the fate of the nation that so many families seek a nonpublic school alternative for their children? There is the notion that a society overdoes what it does best, and, in the process, possibly does itself in. The contemporary apotheosis of school choice may be indicative of a misstep that promotes societal fragmentation, on the one hand, and destroys the public school, on the other.

For school choice to have meaning to those who exercise it, a school must live up to the orientation for which it was chosen, realizing it in curricular and other terms. Unsurprisingly, the same obligation exists in regard to public schools, as I learned when I studied Mansfield High School and its village community (Peshkin, 1978/1994). Its high school graduates attended the smaller state universities, if any, and they were diffident about their academic accomplishments relative to students from suburban schools. But they and their parents loved their school, as they should have: it was shaped to suit them, and it did. A school board composed of natives, mostly farmers, were the agents of community tastes, norms, and values, which they applied to whom they hired to administer, counsel, and teach, and to what they sanctioned regarding the content and manner of instruction.

A comparable process of fitting school to student and student to school is at work in the nonpublic school, as we have seen in the Academy's calculated practices for admitting students and hiring and evaluating teachers. For both students and teachers, there is a self-selection and institutional-selection process by means of which they may seek access, in the first place, and by means of which they may be accepted, in the second. So it is that prospective parents and their children can read in the *Parent–Student Handbook* that the Academy does "not intend to revamp or reorganize our programs or requirements to serve students who are not generally suited to succeed in our rigorous college preparatory program." The school serves notice that it means not to be a school for everyone. And so it is that I hear from a teacher who anticipates leaving: "It's not my climate, my bailiwick," he explains. "In other schools, I didn't make any money but I sure enjoyed myself a lot because I was able to help kids that really needed help, that could be stretched. Here, I don't feel as useful. Most of these students are so motivated."

The Handbook indicates that certain types of students will not fit in the Academy. This teacher indicates that he thinks he does not fit in the Academy. If he leaves, he will be replaced by a teacher who, in addition to the promise of fine teaching skills, is prepared to overwork, tolerate high levels of stress, successfully manage multiple, competing demands for time, and thrive under conditions of relatively rapid change. Teacher and school calculate, respectively, "Do I belong here?" and "Does he or she belong with us?" Parents and children make comparable calculations, as Robert Coles, commenting as parent, implies in his interview with Pearl Rock Kane (1992): "I love Latin and Greek, had 6 years of one and 4 of the other, and I wanted to see my children educated that way. This is what private schools have in the academic sense that is most valuable" (p. 293).

As seen from within, the good fit between the rural school and community I studied did not please everyone. Pleasing everyone is impossible, but in Mansfield there was a mainstream, a predominating constituency, that was comfortable with its modest school. Similarly, Kozol (1991) observed that, "The crowding of the school [he observed] reflects the crowding of the street. 'It becomes striking,' says a parent ... 'how closely these schools reflect their communities, as if the duty of the school were to prepare a child for the life he's born to. ... It hardly seems fair'" (p. 159). For many families, the Academy exists—and thinks it fair that it does—to prepare children for this exact purpose. For many others, it exists to avoid the life they've been born to, an instance of status maintenance, in the first case, and status reversal, in the second.

Institutional Student Choice

The right of students to turn away from their local public school does not include the right to be accepted by the school they seek to enter; that right is reserved by the schools themselves because of the American Value of Institutional Student Choice. In Personal School Choice, I see exercised the value of individual autonomy for the schooling of children. In Institutional Student Choice, I see exercised the value of institutional autonomy in places where schooling is not a matter of the public good but of personal taste, which may or may not contribute to the common good. In this private school domain of personal and institutional choice, there is none of the obligatoriness that prevails in the public domain.

Americans are disposed to think and calculate and rationalize in terms of what we hold to be our rights. We fortify the case for something by dressing it up in the garb of, "That's our right!" I turn to thinking of rights because all along I have wished that some version, some close approximation, of the Academy's opportunities would be available to all American children. However, I turn from this devout wish to the regrettable reality that no one has a right to an Academy education. Nothing in our laws, our court decisions, or our customs, norms, or mores substantiates that such schooling is anyone's right. That some individuals chance to have access to such an education does not thereby establish the right for those who chance not to be so blessed. It is American to believe that the benefits of our institutions, in contrast to the benefits of our laws, need not extend equally to all people. It is unfair and illegal to be cheated in America, but not to suffer. We accept, accordingly, vast differentials in the level of comfort, well-being, and opportunity among our people, the legislative, academic, and journalistic advocates of a more generous safety net never succeeding in carrying the day.[2] When applied to education, this differential is absurd.

As a nation, we began with the constitutional entrenchment of rights that have forever shaped our laws, our institutions, our lives. However, no amount of messing about with the notion of equality of opportunity has ever created warranted grounds for visualizing an Academy-type education as being anyone's right. Philosophers and politicians and economists tangle with some combination of ideas and financial-funding formulas to accommodate the variables that are involved in furthering equality of opportunity. Still, no forthcoming outcome embraces formulations that state it is anyone's right to benefit from a quality of schooling that the Academy routinely, annually provides its students.

There are formulations, however, that struggle with the complexity of school policy, hoping to do justice to the ordinary variability of children that, obviously, militates against providing everyone the same educational experience. Here is an example from a prominent New Zealand educator, the late Clarence Beeby: "Every person ... has a right, as a citizen, to a free education of the kind for which he is best fitted and to the fullest extent of his powers" ("Beeb"-An Intellectual Architect of Modern Education, 1998, p. 12). Beeby's stab at a concise coverall for doing the right thing falters with the roadblock concepts of "best fitted" and "to the fullest extent of his powers." Try to operationalize these notions in the policies and practices of an education system. Meanwhile, states struggle—more often today than in the past—with financial arrangements that respond to the inequities

---

[2]For example, James Pinkerton (1996) cites these statistics from Lipset's book, *American Exceptionalism*: "in 1992 just 38% of Americans agreed that government should reduce the differences in income between rich and poor, compared with 65% of Britons, 66% of West Germans and 80 percent of Italians" (p. 7). Do kindness and justice come in different cultural guises?

that exist among school districts. Still, as a nation we proceed in our public and nonpublic schools as if there is limited space at the top, giving little more than lip service to the wish that all children should have a chance to advance as far as they can.

With the exception of those students whose past familial ties to a particular school guarantee their admission, all other students are at the mercy of the institution's right to choose its students. The reality of this decision may be undermined by a dearth of applicants and, thus, no genuine choice to exercise. Because neither of these two instances apply at the Academy, it enjoys the value of institutional choice.

Extending the American Dream

In 1987, the Academy's Board of Trustees committed itself to a policy that stipulated "no eligible student be denied an education at Edgewood Academy because of financial reasons." Thereby has the school contributed annually, perhaps in perpetuity, to leveling the educational playing field and to the vaunted American Dream, a case of advantage extended. It suitably, if less dramatically, engenders and perpetuates the American Dream for its many students who come from more economically favored homes.

The school's financial policy is shaped by its diversity policy that encourages a dedicated search for academically qualified Native American, African American, and Hispanic American youth. The rationale for these two policies differs among its various supporters, but, clearly, by their implementation the Academy contributes to the cause of equality of educational opportunity. The American Dream is enacted at the Academy for both those who can afford its costs and those who cannot.

As an American Value, the American Dream is a shorthand way to capture our national spirit of optimism about attaining a promising future, of becoming somebody, as might have been said in an earlier day. If we do not have a monopoly on promising futures, we may be the only nation that has named and enshrined the idea. However much it lacks details of quantity and quality, the American Dream is substantive: we understand that someone has been deprived of something of consequence when they are unable to attain some version of the American Dream. And we know that an institution merits commendation when it acts to extend the Dream to those whom it otherwise might elude.

"Helping economically less fortunate others," an institutional way to speak of this American Value, is, as they all are, a disputed one. From a reactionary view, such help is dismissed as unwise, coddling, a decision based on unwarranted guilt and economic confusion. From a Marxist view, Paul Sweezy writes that "prep schools and colleges [play a] dangerous role ... as recruiters for the ruling class, sucking upwards the ablest elements of the lower class and thus performing the double function of infusing new brains into the ruling class and weakening the political leadership of the working class" (quoted in Baltzell, 1964, p. 344). While I never detected the least sense that either coddling or class weakening was anyone's understanding of the Academy's financial and diversity policies, I think Sweezy's observations are not farfetched. For example, Pueblo Indian elders frequently admonished their children, as I learned in the course of another study (Peshkin, 1997), "don't forget who you are and where you come from," a recognition that such forgetting, as Sweezy indicates, is common.

Within groups identified by ethnicity, nationality, or social class, those who have made it are not reputed for remembering their group members who have not. Such back-turning is not a convincing argument for opposing these Academy policies; it does remind us of the potentially high price families and communities may pay when the social mobility of their children is significantly enhanced. The Academy's many financially limited and ethnically diverse students testify to the distance independent schools have traveled from the days when their graduates were almost invariably "soldiers for their class" (Cookson & Persell, 1985, p. 26), "Christian gentlemen who followed the footsteps of their fathers into corporate board rooms with little knowledge of all those Americans who lacked the privilege of a boarding school education" (Armstrong, 1990, p. 15).

The Academy's nonpublic status permits it the liberty to determine how it will allocate its funds. It can avoid the contentiousness of public schools that struggle with some version of distributive justice in the allocation of resources to its students of varied levels of interest, preparedness, and ability to succeed with academic tasks. The particulars of equal educational opportunity play out in the concreteness of a school's distribution of resources. Many parents sidestep the resulting arguments by choosing an elite prep school, preferring not to leave to chance the issue of how or if their children might benefit in a public school. By virtue of their independence, such schools need not struggle over resource allocation. They can focus resources on their students as they wish, and leave the issue of distributive justice to their public counterparts, who must deal with those students who, by some measures, are less interested, less prepared, less able or willing to learn.

Though it is not their intention to do so, nonpublic schools simplify the work of public schools in the matter of equalizing opportunity. They do this by attracting students whose parents are so committed to the rationale of their chosen nonpublic school that if their children attended a public school, they would likely be at odds with it. I saw this happen in fundamentalist Christian schools (Peshkin, 1986), whose doctrine mandated ends and means of schooling that no public institution should dare to satisfy. For these particular Christian parents, equality is notably less the issue than doctrinal fittingness. They can think their children stand on equal footing with other children when they receive the right education in religious terms. Equivalence in financial terms is somewhat important, but not fundamental. The public schools that Christian schoolchildren stay away from have one less major fight to fight. But when these children attend Christian schools, everyone is spared a battle that goes to the heart of a democracy, one that entails working out differences, compromising, learning to live and let live, and the like. The nation pays a price for allowing nonpublic schools to exist; we would pay a higher price by disallowing them.

There are little patches of leveled educational playing fields scattered across the country wherever independent schools have had the means and the will to enroll bright but financially dispossessed students. The ambiguity of such opportunities was epitomized for me in the graduation scene I witnessed. Under the large tent that sheltered the June graduates and their parents, I met the family of the Academy's Stanford-bound Native American student. His younger siblings, currently reservation-school students, were present for this special occasion. None of them, I learned, had yet demonstrated any academic interest or promise; their days in school were a world away from those of their big brother. The Academy graduate, proudly resplendent in his dark, formal robes, was keenly aware of the uncertain course of his cultural remaining and becoming that was shaped by the world of the Academy and Stanford, on the one hand, and of his reservation family and community, on the other. He simultaneously feared that he would lose valued cultural roots, anticipated a continuation of his already exceptional academic victories, and often felt ready to explode from the clashing values and prospects his young life embodied.

Such are the land mines that stud these playing fields! Should they be offered? Are they an opportunity? Would it be better if they did not exist? Can the schools that create these playing fields ever become congenial places for those they welcome to them? Or will they inevitably invite the comment that Hispanic Johanna Vega (1992) made about Groton, the elite Northeastern boarding school from which she graduated: "This place was made for them [rich, White students], not for me" (p. 253). Ironically, neither Groton nor any other such school will get better at making their schools comfortable places for their Johanna Vegas unless they are willing to come and enabled to do so. It is further ironic that much of what makes the Grotons uncomfortable for their Johanna Vegas is exactly what establishes the schools as potential opportunities for them.

Americans like metaphors drawn from sports. I can only reason that a level playing field reflects a past time of poor equipment for making the ground ready for play. Level fields mean that players have an equal chance to succeed on the basis of their merit, unimpeded by external conditions that unequally impact the players. In the case of schooling, such conditions may be the facts of class, ethnicity, and gender. Ambiguity and irony aside, there is something comfortingly positive about the thrust of a school policy that succeeds in bringing children to substantial educational opportunity.

When Edgewood Academy admits its many Johanna Vegas and Stanford-bound Native Americans, it goes against our historical grain by enabling social unequals to be treated equally, giving priority to its students' academic status without regard to their class status. Moreover, the Academy does not just open its doors to these students, it seeks them out, appreciating that they do not naturally and easily come to a school that is so imposing, so redolent of ends and means that are not suitable for them. The distinguished success of the Academy's financial and diversity policies calls attention to the seemingly intractable issue of unequal opportunity and thus to the unlikely realization of the American Dream for so many American children. The unequal reach of success has that evocative potential.

Institutional Advantaging

Institutional Advantaging, another American Value, refers to the process of marking all students by means of a school's particular educational experiences, both formal and informal. The process of marking is common to all schools; it is accentuated in nonpublic schools, where the intention to mark builds on those distinctions the schools advertise to attract its applicants.

As a nation, we value the right of schools to set themselves apart from other schools, to be distinctive in a way that shapes the school experience, on the one hand, and shapes those who undergo this experience, on the other. It is not too farfetched to conclude that nonpublic schools fashion a state of competing advantages (another way of speaking about marking), their victories broadcast in the columns of scores, percentages, and wins and losses, in reference to one or another supposedly measurable indicator of accomplishment.

The Academy concentrates on preparing its students to compete with students from other elite schools from across the entire country in securing advantage and in passing advantage on to their own kin. Accordingly, the Academy may be thought of as providing an exalted rite of mobility passage, more surely stamping its students with the means for getting ahead than most schools in the nation. Year after year, students are prepared and tested, tested and prepared, in the company of peers undergoing the same trial. They begin with the challenge of entry and continue thereafter with the acquisition of skills, habits, and understandings that are requisite for reaching the upper echelons of the American Dream.

This rite of passage embodies a common set of experiences for all Academy students, as I now clarify in a hypothetical example. Each step in the passage incorporates a sense, an awareness, an experience, an accomplishment, or a comparison that bears the potential for congratulation and self-congratulation; taken together the steps comprise the Academy's process of privileging. The preface to the process is "I am an Academy student" so:

- Look at me, I attend the most desirable school around;
- look at my fellow students, the best of the best;
- look at these buildings, the grounds, the equipment, everything—always in order, all first-rate;
- look at the others outside, looking at me and my school;
- look who teaches here—they come from everywhere, competing to get hired just as we compete to get admitted, even PhDs, who could be teaching in colleges and universities;
- look how well the school does—our teams, our clubs, our individual students and teachers—in competitions with schools from throughout the state and the whole country;
- look how well I do, managing a life packed with activities, pressures, requirements, deadlines—and I'm making it;
- look at the colleges and universities that accept me and my classmates—we join the best of the best as we continue our education.

I do not believe this portrait overstates the passage of students from the day they enter the Academy to the day they graduate. Consciousness of this "look at me," "look at us" experience is greater or lesser for some students because of their greater capacity for self-awareness or their social class starting point. It remains for all a shared process with each of its distinguishing aspects proclaiming both "here is what happened" and, in addition, "consider the meaning of what happened."

The Academy is an effective agent of hierarchical distinctions. It would consider itself at fault if the experiences it provided students did not distinguish—and elevate—them relative to others. "Hierarchy," wrote anthropologist Richard Shweder (1991), is "a concomitant of excellence" (p. 35), and excellence is the stock-in-trade of elite schools. Their educational achievements contribute to hierarchical distinctions that later will be based, as well, on economic accumulation and political power. Clearly, American schools dispense education primarily for its utility in society beyond the school. As a result, those who fight the cause of emphasizing learning for its own sake and diminishing the focus on grades, transcript packing, and college-admission success have the odds stacked against them. Our dominant pragmatic side is responsive to the instrumental payoff of schooling; as a nation, we convert forms of educational experience into occupational and social success. Our less-respected intellectual side is responsive to consummatory payoff, of learning as its own reward, of learners moved by the joy of accomplishment. In practice,

Academy teachers attend to both the instrumental and the consummatory; they have to. To focus exclusively on the former would threaten their personal attachment to the life of the mind; to focus exclusively on the latter would deny the determination of parents and students to be prepared for their future life. In practice, while ambiguity is now and again voiced, the pragmatists have the upper hand (see Pope, 1999).

PERMISSIBLE ADVANTAGE

The aforementioned American Values implicate the matter of Permissible Advantage.[3] This notion captures the tension between the belief that there is something unfair and unseemly about advantage and the understanding that it is an unavoidable fact of life. It takes very little experience to understand that life is unfair, and that we will be eternally challenged to understand and accept unfairness, which is the advantage from which we do not personally benefit. The point here is about our acceptance of, if not our belief in, educational advantages that accrue unevenly in favor of some people relative to most others. Over time, we come to acknowledge this uneven distribution as normal, accepting some advantages as permissible, others as not. Indeed, to come to terms with this uneven distribution, we develop elaborate rationales that resonate with premises, logic, arguments, even data and doctrines.

What schools like Edgewood Academy suggest is that it is virtuous to accumulate educational wealth, just as it is virtuous to accumulate financial wealth. As a capitalist society, we are disposed to think that there is no legal or moral limit to what one can acquire and hold on to. The Academy exemplifies this "virtue." Moreover, there is neither legal nor moral limit to either the financial or the educational wealth any nonpublic school can acquire. There is no educational equivalent of antitrust legislation, and there is no chance of any single school creating a monopoly or doing in the competition. That the graduates of one school regularly outperform the graduates of most other schools may be grounds for envy but not for a lawsuit, at least not yet. Our national proclivity, such as it is, favors pulling up those who suffer a competitive disadvantage, rather than diminishing the advantages of the advantaged. "Pulling up," to say the least, is a contested matter, as is the expression itself. It is easier to concede that disadvantage exists than to know what to do about it.

To affirm that not everyone seeks the putative advantages of an elite prep school is to state the obvious. To affirm that the students of such schools are advantaged is no less to claim the obvious. But it is not the advantage side of the term *Permissible Advantage* that needs discussing, it is the permissible side.

---

[3]This idea was developed in conversation with Professor Walter Feinberg, philosopher of education at the University of Illinois.

The case for permissibility, at one level, is syllogistically simple: Nonpublic schools (barring those for witches) are legal. Edgewood Academy is a nonpublic school. Therefore ... Our qualms about privilege and advantage, if we are to have them, must come on grounds other than legality.

One such ground is how, in the first place, a student gains access to the school's advantages. This, too, is a simple matter, for the Academy can make its own rules for admission, and if it applies its rules uniformly to all applicants, it satisfies all the conditions that currently prevail for admission. Outsiders may quarrel with the particulars of admission policy, applying external standards to this critical process, but nonpublic schools rightfully establish their own admission policies.

A second ground is educational. It raises questions about the quality of the students' educational experience. By my standards, I find no basis here for doubting the permissibility of the school's advantage. The teachers are smart, dedicated, and creative; they take their work seriously; they care a great deal about the quality of their students' work. They assign a lot of work, they have very high standards, and they expect the completion of this work at these high standards. Yes, one might ask for something more or different, but that is only to say that teachers, like researchers, never are as good as someone, somewhere thinks they should be.

Another ground is the moral one, and it is not simple. The Academy need not respond, as, in fact, it does, to broadening the base of acceptable students to include those who are academically eligible but lack financial means to pay tuition. When permissibility on moral grounds is applied to admission to the halls of advantage, I am satisfied here, too. Both the procedure itself and the results of the procedure speak to the morality of Academy conduct.

When the moral yardstick is applied to the thornier matter of what Academy students do with their lives, the case becomes most complex, perhaps hopelessly so, given that the least examined aspect of any school is what becomes of its students 10, 20, or 30 years later. It is at least tacitly understood by everyone interested in schools, laypersons and professionals alike, that school effects are tangled and enmeshed in an ever-expanding array of formal and informal experiences. Thus, the farther students get from their school life, the more impossible it becomes to identify what outcomes can be attributable to that life. Yet, if there is one ground on which critics of elite schools stand, including those from within its fold, it is the moral one that "to act morally is to act in terms of the collective interest" (Durkheim, 1925/1961, p. 59). Do Academy students act morally in the collective interest of their community and society? If they do, it is not because their school invests much in their learning to do so.

Perhaps no more than other schools, the Academy develops the efficacy of students on behalf of themselves, for their personal needs, interests, and goals.

This is not done in the sense that students are taught to concentrate on their own good; it is more a matter of what, essentially, is left undone or unsaid that leads me to this conclusion. This relates to what many writers have identified as the country's excessive turn to an individualism that is untempered by a commitment to community. Philosopher Charles Taylor (1991) called this "the dark side of individualism," a form unmitigated by any serious effort to introduce students to the imperatives of responsibility (p. 4).[4]

In his exploration of individualism, Taylor informs us that it was an extraordinarily valuable quality for promoting the freedom that resounds in the modern world. When, however, individualism lacks a "moral principle" that can "offer some view on how the individual should live with others" (1991, p. 45), people end up, as he aptly quotes de Tocqueville to say, "enclosed in their own hearts" (1991, p. 9). It becomes a principle oriented to narcissism, to a "culture of self-fulfillment" (1991, p. 15).

An Academy that functions in the service of individualism, as several of its teachers mentioned, is a school, unsurprisingly, in the service of capitalism. This, as many writers on social reproduction have observed,[5] is its natural orientation as an American school; it is every American school's default identity, what it will become unless there is an intended, concerted thrust to the contrary. Educators do not apologize for their schools doing what comes naturally, although, as we have heard, many Academy educators are uneasy about the magnitude of their institution's capacity to facilitate their students' passage to personal success relative to its capacity to promote the common good.

A moral yardstick applied to nonpublic schools invites attention to a possible conflict of values—the freedom to establish schools that honor difference contending with the need for national unity. To be sure, neither the Academy nor its fellow nonpublic schools are replete with aberrant Americans who chafe at their association with an unacceptable American identity. Moreover, there is much beyond schooling that socializes youth to nonlocal, nonpersonal commitments. The hazard of "fragmentation," as Charles Taylor clarifies, can arise from the ways some nonpublic schools intend to differentiate their students.

---

[4]Derek Bok (1996) made a similar point in *The State of the Nation*, as did Robert Bellah, William Sullivan, Ann Swidler, and Steven Tipton, most emphatically, long before him in their 1985 book, *Habits of the Heart*: "The tension between self-reliant competitive enterprise and a sense of public solidarity ... has been the most important unresolved problem in American history ... " (1985, p. 256). Speaking from the perspective of her book on rights, law professor Mary Ann Glendon (1991) focused on our abiding value conflict "between freedom and responsibility, individualism and community, present needs and future plans ... " (p. xii–xiii). On this important issue, see also Lipset's (1995) *American Exceptionalism*, MacIntyre's (1981) *After Virtue: A Study in Moral Theory*, and Peters's (1967) *Ethics and Education*.

[5]For example, see Apple (1982); Bowles and Gintis (1976); Bourdieu and Passeron (1977); and Carnoy and Levin (1985).

Examples are schools whose fundamentalist religious focus claims a Truth that leaves no room for compromise, and that turns belief into clubs for use on would-be detractors. Elite boarding schools are another example, though much less extreme than the former.

By fragmentation Taylor (1991) refers to "a people increasingly less capable of forming a common purpose and carrying it out … as less and less bound to their fellow citizens in common projects and allegiances … linked in partial groupings rather than the whole society" (pp. 112–113). Clearly, the Academy does not advocate fragmentation in any way. Its contribution to this undesirable condition is an artifact of the isolation of its students from others (which happens in all elite public schools, as well), and of its privileging capacity, the basis for its distinctiveness. To be, and mean to be, distinguished, is to engender fragmentation—"less and less bound to their fellow citizens"—even if less powerfully than at some other schools.

The logic that brings me to this point must be tempered by an acknowledgement that American schools generally and unwittingly contribute to fragmentation by their predisposition to focus on the personal interests of students and parents, often to the neglect of the collective interests of society. The considerable advantage of Academy students touches permissibility on the further moral matter of whether the students transform their advantage into a shield of indifference by means of which they ignore or deny the unfairness of inequality. To do so would be to live a comfortable life while sanctioning the hardship of others, a pernicious outcome that the Academy does not condone. That some Academy teachers want their students to eschew the narcissistic individualism so disturbing to Taylor is evidenced by a question one teacher asked on the year-end American History final exam. For 50 points, half the total, the exam required students to write an essay on "The American Dream." One section of the essay invited students to consider, "As a member of the Academy community invested in diversity, what does the American Dream mean to you now? How does your American Dream compare with the traditional one(s)? How does your dream compare with the dreams of other Americans?"

I like this question, and I respect what I believe are the teacher's intentions by asking it. I'd feel more assured if Academy students were steeped in such experiences. Their education need not give or promise solutions to problems, but it should leave them knowing that the suffering of the least of us is an intolerable indignity, a war being lost that should be seen as the best of all wars to win, the war for the common good. Permissible advantage—what is acceptable, and impermissible advantage—what is not, may more likely be the consideration of philosophers and policymakers than of adolescent students and their teachers. But what constitutes permissibility and impermissiblity should be a premise of pedagogical and curricular considerations by all students and schools everywhere.

Drawn earlier to the half-empty cup of American children, I return to the Academy's abundant cup and its expressed devotion to excellence. While all schools should attend seriously to giving back, taking responsibility, and committing to the public good, the Academy could be expected to firmly place these matters within their domain of excellence, and undertake learning how to master them.

To allow the college factor to dwarf all else that it does, as I believe is the case, is to cast serious doubt on the permissibility of its advantage on moral grounds. The Academy's gift of plenty and its enabling concomitants argue for its unique opportunity to learning how to direct students to good citizenship, to moving them beyond the clichés that too often are associated with the marginal curricular activity called "civics."

A woman writing in her newspaper's letters to the editor section mentions almost choking on her morning coffee when she learned what was happening in a nearby suburban Chicago school: "How can [they] waste tax money teaching kids how to groom dogs when many inner-city schools can't afford new textbooks? ... [And how can they] justify a bowling alley, when many poor children ... [don't have] breakfast before school?" (Colton, 1992, p. 10). In so many words, good-citizen Colton urges her readers to feel "the added pressure of having to fulfill a moral obligation" (Uchitelle, 1997, p. 38). The essential concern raised by my study of Edgewood Academy is about moral obligations, so that I ask, as I urge others to ask, Is it fair? Is it just? Is it good? that we have such schools that lie a chasm beyond those that most American children attend? Does their thriving presence hold implications for what we ought to do as educators, citizens, politicians, policymakers?

The Institutional Advantaging manifested by the operation of a privileged school converges on a single point: the injustice of inequality. The issue is less what the Academy can do for its students, than what it does that happens too seldom for students in the rest of the country. In short, inequality and injustice are the counterpoint of the privilege, advantage, and opportunity that Edgewood Academy symbolizes. In previous chapters, I have tried to make clear what is celebratory about the Academy. But it is on the school as a manifestation of educational privilege, not of academic excellence, that I focus. With advantage as my chosen lens, I can ask Is it fair? Is it just? Is it good? that so few students are favored relative to so many others.

Jonathon Kozol (1992) quoted an unnamed Black principal: "So we accept some things and we forget some other things and what we can't forget we learn how to shut out of mind and we adopt the rhetoric that is required of us and we speak of 'quality' or 'excellence'—not justice" (1992, p. 152).

Speaking of justice is what the soul of America most particularly ought to be about.

References

Apple, M. (1982). *Education and power*. Boston: Routledge & Kegan Paul.

Armstrong, C. F. (1990). On the making of good men: Character-building in the New England boarding schools. In P. W. Kingston & L. S. Lewis (Eds.), *The high status track*. Albany: State University of New York Press.

Baltzell, D. E. (1964). *The Protestant establishment: Aristocracy and caste in America*. New York: Random House.

Bauman, Z. (1995). *Life in fragments: Essays in postmodern morality*. Oxford, England: Blackwell.

"Beeb" an intellectual architect of modern education. (1998, April–June). *IIEP Newsletter*, 12–13.

Bellah, R., Sullivan, W. M., Swidler, A., & Tipton, S. M. (1985). *Habits of the heart*. New York: Harper & Row.

Bellah, R., Sullivan, W. M., Swidler, A., & Tipton, S. M. (1991). *The good society*. New York: Knopf.

Bills, D. B. (1988, January). Educational credentials and promotions: Does schooling do more than get you in the door? *Sociology of Education, 61*, 52–60.

Bok, D. (1996). *The state of the nation: Government and the quest for a better society*. Cambridge, MA: Harvard University Press.

Bourdieu, P., & Passeron, J. C. (1977). *Reproduction: In education, society, and power*. Beverly Hills, CA: Sage.

Bowles, S., & Gintis, H. (1976). *Schooling in capitalist America*. New York: Basic Books.

Bresler, M. (1991). Review of *The high-status track* by Paul Kingston and Lionel Lewis. *Contemporary Sociology, 20*(6), 867–868.

Carnoy, M., & Levin, H. M. (1985). *Schooling and work in the democratic state*. Stanford, CA: Stanford University Press.

Cassidy, J. (1998, November 30). Profile: Height of eloquence. *New Yorker*, 70–75.

Cassidy, J. (1999, March 8). The firm. *New Yorker*, 28–36.

Clark, C. (1991). Real lessons for imaginary teachers. *Journal of Curriculum Studies, 23*(5), 429–433.

Coleman, J. S. (1988). Social capital, human capital, and schools. *Independent School, 48*(1), 9–16.

Coles, R. (1992). Teaching social responsibility: An interview with Robert Coles. In P. R. Kane (Ed.), *Independent schools, independent thinkers*. San Francisco: Jossey-Bass.

Collins, R. (1979). *The credential society*. New York: Academic Press.

Colton, K. (1992, October 10). Onus for education equality on all of U.S. *Chicago Tribune*, p. 10.

Conway, G. E. (1992). School choice: A private school perspective. *Phi Delta Kappan, 73*(7), 561–563.

Cookson, P. W. Jr., & Persell, C. H. (1985). *Preparing for power: America's elite boarding schools*. New York: Basic Books.

Deal, T. E. (1992). School culture: Balancing tradition and innovation. In Pearl Rock Kane (Ed.), *Independent schools, independent thinkers*. San Francisco: Jossey-Bass.

Devins, N. E. (Ed.). (1989). *Public values, private schools*. London, England: Falmer.

Dewey, J. (1909). *Moral principles in education*. Carbondale: Southern Illinois University Press.

Dewey, J. (1927). *The public and its problems*. New York: Henry Holt.

Dickstein, M. (1996, April 4). Moral fiction. *New York Times Book Review*, p. 19.

Doyle, D. P. (1981). A din of inequity: Private schools reconsidered. *Teachers College Record, 82*(4), 661–673.

Durkheim, E. (1961). *Moral education: A study in theory and application of the sociology of education*. New York: Free Press. (Original work published 1925).

Educational Policies Commission. (1963). *Social responsibility in a free society*. Washington, DC: National Education Association.

Galbraith, J. K. (1969). *The affluent society*. (2nd ed.). Boston: Houghton Mifflin.

Glendon, M. A. (1991). *Rights talk: The impoverishment of political discourse*. New York: Free Press.

Goffman, E. (1961). *Asylums: Essays on the social situation of mental patients and other inmates*. Garden City, NY: Anchor Books.

Greeley, A. (1993). Bricolage among the trash cans. *Society, 30*(2), 70–75.

Haertel, E., James, T., & Levin, H. M. (1987). *Comparing public and private schools*. (Vol. 2). Philadelphia: Falmer.

Hays, K. (1994). *Practicing virtues: Moral traditions at Quaker and military boarding schools*. Berkeley: University of California Press.

Heely, A. V. (1951). *Why the private school?* New York: Harper & Brothers.

Jackson, P. W., Boostrom, R. E., & Hansen, D. T. (1993). *The moral life of schools*. San Francisco: Jossey-Bass.

James, T., & Levin, H. M. (1988). *Comparing public and private schools: Vol. 1. Institutions and organizations*. New York: Falmer.

Kagan, J. (1998). *Three seductive ideas*. Cambridge, MA: Harvard University Press.

Kaminsky, M. (1992). Introduction. In *Remembered lives* by Barbara Myerhoff. Ann Arbor: University of Michigan Press.

Kane, P. R. (1991). Independent schools in American education. *Teachers College Record, 92*(3), 396–408.

Kemerer, F. R. (1992, January 8). The publicization of the private school. *Education Week*, 56–42.

Kingston, P. W. (1981). The credential elite and the credential route to success. *Teachers College Record, 82*(4), 589–600.

Kingston, P. W., & Lewis, L. (Eds.). (1990). *The high-status track: Studies of elite schools and stratification*. Albany: State University of New York Press.

Kozol, J. (1991). *Savage inequalities*. New York: Harper-Collins.

Lemann, N. (1997, September). The SAT meritocracy. *The Washington Monthly*, 32–36.

Lipset, S. (1995). *American exceptionalism*. New York: Norton.

Lukas, J. (1998). *A thread of years*. New Haven: Yale University Press.

MacIntyre, A. (1981). *After virtue: A study in moral theory*. Notre Dame, IN: University of Norte Dame Press.

McLachlan, J. (1970). *American boarding schools: A historical study*. New York: Charles Scribner & Sons.

Maxwell, J. D., & Maxwell, M. P. (1995). The reproduction of class in Canada's elite independent schools. *British Journal of Sociology of Education, 16*(3), 309–326.

Meier, D. (1995, April 19). Democracy is not always convenient. *Education Week, 35*–36.

Myths and facts about private school choice. (1993, Fall). *American Educator*.

Nader, L. (1969). Up the anthropologist—perspectives gained from studying up. In D. Hymes (Ed.), *Reinventing anthropology*. New York: Vintage Books.

Olson, L. (1993, December 15). Who's afraid of O.B.E.? *Education Week*, 25–27.

Pagans want vouchers for a witchcraft school. (1993, July 16). *The New Mexican*, p. A5.

Parssinen, C. A. (1982). Social explorers and social scientists: The dark continent of Victorian ethnography. In J. Ruby (Ed.), *A crack in the mirror*. Philadelphia: University of Pennsylvania Press.

Persell, C. H., & Cookson, P. W. (1982). Characterizing and bartering: Elite education and social reproduction. In P. W. Kingston & L. Lewis (Eds.), *The high-status track: Studies of elite schools and stratification*. Albany: State University of New York Press.

Peshkin, A. (1994). *Growing up American: Schooling and the survival of community*. Chicago: University of Chicago Press. (Original work published 1978).

Peshkin, A. (1982). *The imperfect union: School consolidation and community conflict*. Chicago: University of Chicago Press.

Peshkin, A. (1986). *God's choice: The total world of a fundamentalist Christian school*. Chicago: University of Chicago Press.

Peshkin, A. (1991). *The color of strangers, the color of friends*. Chicago: University of Chicago Press.

Peshkin, A. (1995). The complex world of an embedded institution: Schools and their constituent publics. In L. C. Rigsby, M. C. Reynolds, & M. C. Wang (Eds.), *School-community connections: Exploring issues for research and practice*. San Francisco: Jossey-Bass.

Peshkin, A. (1997). *Places of memory: Whiteman's schools and Native American communities*. Mahwah, NJ: Lawrence Erlbaum Associates.

Peters, R. S. (1967). Ethics and education. Atlanta: Scott, Foresman & Company.

Pinkerton, J. P. (1996, February 11). Not just another country. *New York Times Book Review*, p. 7.

Pope, D. C. (1999). *Doing school: "Successful" students' experiences of the high school curriculum*. Unpublished doctoral dissertation, Stanford University, Stanford, California.

Powell, A. G. (1996). *Lessons from privilege: The American prep school tradition*. Cambridge, MA: Harvard University Press.

Proweller, A. (1998). *Constructing female identities: Meaning making in an upper middle class youth culture*. Albany: State University of New York Press.

Rorty, R. (1989). *Contingency, irony and solidarity*. Cambridge, England: Cambridge University Press.

Sandham, J. L. (1998, November 4). Halfway home. *Education Week*, 36–41.

Schmoker, M. (1992, May 13). What schools can learn from Toyota of America. *Education Week*, 23–25.

Shweder, R. A. (1991, March 17). Dangerous thoughts. *New York Times Book Review*, pp. 1, 30, 31, 35.

Simons, G. (1992). Diversifying independent schools: Examples from the prep for prep program. In P. R. Kane (Ed.), *Independent schools, independent thinkers*. San Francisco: Jossey-Bass.

State must run adequate public schools. (1997). *Illinois Brief, 54*(2), 2.

Taylor, C. (1991). *The ethics of authenticity.* Cambridge, MA: Harvard University Press.

Tom, A. (1984). *Teaching as a moral craft.* New York: Longman.

Uchitelle, L. (1997, December 23). Opportunity lost. *New York Times Book Review*, p. 38.

Top ten universities. (1995, April 7). *U. S. News and World Report.*

Vega, J. (1992). From the South Bronx to Groton. In P. R. Kane (Ed.), *Independent schools, independent thinkers*, San Francisco: Jossey-Bass.

Walsh, M. (1999, March 17). Ground zero for vouchers. *Education Week*, 47–51.

Webster's Third New International Dictionary. (1966). Springfield, MA: G. C. Merriam Company.

Weis, L., & Fine, M. (1992, Winter). The need for research on "silencing." *American Educational Research Association Newsletter* [Division G].

Author Index

Subject Index